IT'S NOT JUST PUPPIES AND KITTENS

It's Not Just Puppies and Kittens: Behind the Scenes With a Small Animal Vet
It's Not Just Puppies and Kittens: Behind the Scenes With a Small Animal Vet
It's Not Just Puppies and Kittens: Behind the Scenes With a Small Animal Vet
It's Not Just Puppies and Kittens. . . .
    It's Not Just Puppies and Kittens. . . .
    It's Not Just Puppies and Kittens. . . .
        It's Not Just Puppies. . . .
        It's Not Just Puppies. . . .
        It's Not Just Puppies. . . .
            's Not Just Puppies. . . .
            's Not Just Puppies. . . .
            's Not Just Puppies. . . .

                's Not Puppies. . . .
                's Not Puppies. . . .
                's Not Puppies. . . .
                    'sNot Puppies
                    'sNot Puppies
                    'sNot Puppies
                        'sNot Pup 1

It's Not Just Puppies and Kittens

It's Not Just
Puppies
and
Kittens

Behind the Scenes with a Small Animal Vet

by MJ Wixsom, DVM MS

It's Not Just Puppies and Kittens
C Guardian A Publishing

Copyright © 2015 by MJ Wixsom
All rights reserved. No part of this publication may be reproduced, distributed, or transmitted in any form or by any means, including photocopying, recording, or other electronic or mechanical methods, without the prior written permission of the publisher, except in the case of brief quotations embodied in critical reviews and certain other noncommercial uses permitted by copyright law. For permission requests, write to the publisher, addressed "Attention: Permissions Coordinator," at the address below.
C Guardian A Press
918 Bellefonte Road
Flatwoods, KY 41139
www.GuardianAnimal.com
Ordering Information:
Quantity sales. Special discounts are available on quantity purchases by corporations, associations, and others. For details, contact the publisher at the address above.

Printed in the United States of America
First Printing, 2015
ISBN 9780997025781

Dedication

To my clients, they make everything possible.
Especially the clients who said I should write a book.

And to a favorite client: Nikki, keep fighting!

And

To my patients, they make everything fun.

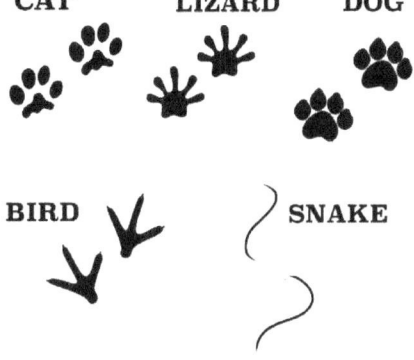

Author's Acknowledgments

'sNot Puppies would not be possible without my support crew!

Thank you to my staff who do their jobs so that I can write and do my day job.

Most of these articles first ran in The Greenup Beacon. I now write for the Sunday Ironton Tribune and About Greenup Magazine. Thank you to Hank, Mike, Michelle and Cathie for your support over the years. Without writing weekly with deadlines, 'sNot Puppies never would have happened.

Thank you to my writing group who encourage me and correct my grammar, even if it is after I just paid for the new cover design.

Thank you Fiverr folks for friendships, illustrations (Maria Yousaf: section digitized prints and Mahesh Ambawattha, a young MD, from Sir Lanka: story illustrations) and a cover.

Thank you Jean, Chris, Matt and Cathie who edited and added those pesky grammar things. And commas. Math and science are easy. They have rules. Commas have no rules. Well, not that I ever could figure out. But if I missed a correction they sent, email me at snotpup@gmail.com and I will fix it and send you a thank you note.

Thank you to my best friend, Julia, who had to read all of these articles in the raw form. Sometimes I tested her resolve for tact and she would tell me I could put an article in the book, but not in the paper at that time. So, a few articles are brand new to "The Book," because it is finally here. I do make her laugh, though. And I teach her things she doesn't need to know.

Thank you to my family who put up with me not being at home or always late because I am writing or checking back in on patients. I love you both. Yes, M'Kinzy, even more than the Labrador Retrievers. And thanks Matt, who always has my back, so I can do crazy stuff.

It's Not Just Puppies and Kittens

Foreword

From the airline conversations I have had, it would seem virtually everyone wanted to be a veterinarian at some point in their life. After all, vets spend their days with animals and don't have to work with people. They fix all animals and are always heroes. Although neither statement is completely true, the impression is that veterinarians have great and high paying jobs. Regardless, few people make the sacrifices to go to veterinary school and fewer stay in practice. Because no matter how it seems, being a veterinarian is a lot of work and stress. There is a huge variety of species and biological systems that must be known. A veterinarian must be a gynecologist, ophthalmologist, internal medicine specialist, endocrinologist, surgeon, oncologist, physical therapist, dentist, behaviorist and, at times, human counselor. And just when you have the dog's cardiac disease treatment down, a three chambered heart of a snake needs help. Or ferret. Or cat or pig, or... And mistakes can mean lives.

The high stress reality is that of all the health care professionals, veterinarians have the highest suicide rate. It takes the right mix of intelligence, compassion, business sense and knowledge to be a successful, happy veterinarian. Nobody goes into veterinary medicine to be rich, but veterinarians are people, too. The knowledge of animal care mixes with humanity to find a commonality we all share.

I started writing a weekly newspaper column simply to educate about animals and their care. But beyond teaching about animals, there is the very real human side of animal care. People were more interested in what happens behind the scenes with the many trials and tribulations and simple raw humanity of veterinary medicine. This is the journey that became interesting, because we are all people with feelings and responsibility. In short, veterinary medicine really is much more than just playing with puppies and kittens all day.

But like the intensity of veterinary medicine, 'sNot Puppies is meant to be taken one day at a time, not in one reading or setting. Read a story or two, then set it aside and enjoy your pets. Come back later to learn a little more.

Disclaimer

I am not a specialist. Unless you are a client, I have not examined your pet. This is good information, but very subtle symptoms can change the entire outcome of a case. That is why I am not a big Dr. Google fan. YOUR veterinarian is your best option. If we are in your area, we hope it is us. If we are not nearby, there is someone who is that can help you!

BTW Sometimes I have changed names of patients to ease pain or protect identities. Sometimes a story needs a few extra details to be a good story. Regardless, everything in the articles has happened sometime to someone or some critter.

Author's Note:

I believe that words become our thoughts and actions. Therefore I try hard not to participate in the sexist marginalization of current pronouns. Likewise, I cannot refer to a pet as an "it". Since a combination neuter pronoun does not yet exist, I shall in various places use the singular "they" in illogical noun/pronoun places.

I do rant occasionally for the combination of She/He/IT, but to use it would not be sensitive and would detract more than they or it.

SECTION 1: SPEAKING OF PETS	12
Dogs, We Can't Even Talk Without Them	13
My Pet Gets Me	15
SECTION 2: ANIMAL CARE	18
Huxley is beyond fat	19
So, How Much Should Huxley Weigh?	22
Ew! Don't Kiss Me!	25
Thunder! Lightning! Fear!	28
Hot Dog? Not Cool!	31
No pain, still gain.	34
I'm sick. Hold the antibiotics.	36
Yapper is having puppies!	39
Death and Dying	41
What is Toxic?	43
I just put a puppy to sleep	45
A Box by the Front Door	48
SECTION 3: ANIMAL DISEASES	51
Roxie is Sick. Really Sick.	52
Canine Distemper	54
Rabies! Oh, No!	57
Remember Izzy?	60
HGE	62

Pyometria	65
If It Had Been a Snake...	67
What Was That?	69
I Touched her Heart	72
SECTION 4: CATS ARE NOT LITTLE DOGS	74
Toxoplasmosis	75
Feline Infectious Peritonitis	78
Old Skinny Cats	80
SECTION 5: PARASITES	82
How Did this Flea Get Here?	83
My Dog Still Has Fleas	85
My dog is Crawling with Fleas!	87
SECTION 6: WILDLIFE	91
Motherhood in the Animal Kingdom	92
There is No Daycare in the Wild.	94
I Have a Bat in My Pocket	96
What Makes Me Cry...	98
Changing Colors	100
SECTION 7: VET LIFE	102
I Woke up to a Bad Dream this Morning, a...	103
What a day!	106
I Went to School for a Long Time to do this	109
The One that Got Away!	111

Please, Don't Pray for Patience for me! ... 114
Do I Need to Worry? ... 116
I Miss my Technology 118
Beck is Going to Germany. ... 121
Have You Ever Treated . . . ? ... 124
Answers to the Fourth Graders ... 127
To Sleep–Forever ... 130

SECTION 8: OUT AND ABOUT ... 134
The 2011 Race to the Sky Sled Dog Race is Over 135
Seal Skin Hat ... 137
Remember Y2K? ... 139
The Scenes are Horrifying. ... 141
The Day the World Changed ... 143

SECTION 9: HOWL-I-DAYS ... 146
The Time Changed. I Haven't yet. ... 147
Make Mine Chocolate ... 149
Yappy Howlidays! Hold the Tinsel ... 151
A Gift for Spot and Tabby ... 154
Twas the Night before Christmas Poem ... 156
Yappy Howl-I-daze! ... 160
Roles and Goals ... 164

MJ WIXSOM, DVM MS MBA ... 167
Dr. Mahesh Ambawattha ... 170

If You Want to Help ... 171
ASK YOUR VETERINARIAN ... 173

It's Not Just Puppies and Kittens

SECTION 1: SPEAKING OF PETS

Dogs, We Can't Even Talk Without Them

The human animal bond is very strong. They comfort us, protect us and live for us. We in return, have dog metaphors throughout our language. Just think about all the ways the four-legged canine animal came into our language.

The word dog can be used with business, dance, failure, finance, follow, friend, horse racing, latch, lumbering, man, private parts, feet, transportation or as a verb.

The alpha male is the leader of the pack, but if I can't teach him to heel, he will spend considerable time in the dog house especially if he is not house trained. If he doesn't step in it, he might get to stay in the pup tent otherwise it might be to the dog pound. But work like a dog, because everyone knows you can't teach a dog new tricks and if you don't have a job you may become a booze hound.

I have a bone to pick which can lead to a bone of contention, but don't bite the hand that feeds you. But if you do throw the dog a bone, you might find it is a dog eat dog world because people act like a dog with a bone and sometimes they just fight like cats and dogs. Or are they just nipping at your heels, because they don't have a dog in this fight?

A dog's bark is worse than his bite, but he is not a lap dog and if you don't put a muzzle on it, it could lead to a real dogfight. So keep them on a short leash or better yet, call off the dogs. And anyway, who, who let the dogs out?

He missed the dog leg in the trail, so he is barking up the wrong tree, but he still has to jump through hoops because he is not as lucky as a dog.

In a bird dog minute you can be a dog's age old and sick as a dog then you die like a dog because it is a dog's life. Maybe you can just play dead. Regardless it is not over until the last dog dies.

Every dog has his day and every day has dog especially in the dog days of August. But if you do die make sure you have your dogtags.

Remember to take a doggie bag for the dog's breakfast or the dog's dinner or are you just eating your own dog food when you really prefer to eat a hot dog.

If you had a hangdog or dogface expression, you would not say "hotdoggity dog." If you were pretty as a speckled pup you might wear a poodle skirt and get Orion's dog star named after you.

This really just sounds like a dog and pony show, so put on the dog. But don't send the dog catcher after the dog wagon.

Kids use the excuse that the dog ate their homework, so they have time for puppy love. And it is okay because on the internet, nobody knows you're a dog.

Adult versions have to do with female dogs, body parts, styles and probably more I really don't want to know about.

My favorite this Friday afternoon of an "interesting" week comes because I do not have a leash and cannot be kept on a leash, so "don't whiz on my leg and tell me it's raining."

Don't think I am hotdogging it, because much of the information for this article came from **http://www.metaphordogs.org**

My Pet Gets Me

We all know people who talk to their pets and many times in a baby talk kind of way. But did you know many pets can understand and attach meaning to words?

Alex, the African Grey parrot, had a vocabulary of more than 150 words at the time of his death at age 30. Dr. Pepperberg, who worked with Alex, said Alex could identify 50 different objects and recognize quantities up to six. Alex could distinguish seven colors and five shapes. Alex understood the concepts of "bigger," "smaller," "same," and "different," and was learning "over" and "under."

Koko, a lowland gorilla, has learned signs for more than a thousand words. She will even combine signs to make new words. Eye-hat is used to describe glasses and a ring becomes a finger-bracelet.

We have known for years that dogs can understand commands. Sit, stay and down help us live with our dogs. But a recent study proved border collies could respond to more than 150 words. This doesn't have to be words that are repeated time after time to be taught. Dogs can pick up on things they just hear.

Isaac, my wonderful yellow Labrador, had never been taught the word "office." But one day as I was coming through the lobby of the office, someone needed me. I opened the door to the back and told Isaac "office." Half an hour later, I found him in my office. Well, actually, his butt was on the carpet and his front feet were in the hallway, his definition of "office." He had even opened two doors to get to the office.

Recently Ranger taught me he can understand things also. Matt had been out of town and we need some powdered milk for wildlife rehab animals. I had called Matt to find out where it was after last year's use. He told me and I repeated it back to him. I did not get the milk, because I knew I would have time in the morning and it was late. That night, Ranger got up in the middle of the night, did not wake me up and snuck down to the kitchen. He reached behind some things to pick up the bag of milk replacer and proceeded to eat it all. Now the milk replacer had been sitting in that exact spot for the past eight to nine months. At no time had he shown the least amount of interest in it. But that night after hearing me repeat back to Matt about it, he headed up a midnight raid and ate every speck.

And there is Bella, who runs and hides and pretends to be asleep when her owners call her for bed. This illusion is somewhat hampered by the fact that she leaves one eye open.

(By the way, I think cats understand, but there is no way a cat is going to cooperate in the laboratory!)

Now dogs probably do not understand abstract concepts. Love, hate and various beliefs do not relate to specific objects or actions. The abstract "I love you" may not mean as much as "treat." Of course, we really do not know how to interpret a dog's mind, so we don't know for sure.

But we all know dogs can seem to completely understand us. Some research had shown dogs can pick up on gestures and cues much better than any other animal. So some of that understanding may be reading our body language or tone of voice. Whatever, my last staff understood this. When I was not in a great frame of mind, they would let Isaac out of his cage and quietly send him up to me. He would insist his head had to be in my lap and I would feel a little less upset about whatever patient had just been lost. I don't care if they understand words or just understand me; either way, I love them.

SECTION 2: ANIMAL CARE

Huxley is Beyond Fat

Huxley is my friends' cat and unfortunately, pets are not the only ones that are fat. The Wall Street Journal's "Our Big Problem" is an article on American obesity.

Obesity is not just unsightly, it is a medical condition. Excess body fat accumulates and then has a negative effect on health and well being.

Obesity reduces life expectancy and increases health problems.

My friends are nearing retirement and have worked hard to lose some weight, but when I first started visiting, their cat was morbidly obese.

My friends described Huxley as fat. I think they were even taken a little aback when I said Huxley was morbidly obese or the equivalent of a 400 to 600-pound person.

The first twenty percent of weight gain is defined as overweight. Then obesity is traditionally defined as 20-40% or more over the ideal weight. Mildly obese is 40-100% above your idea weight. But more than 100% of your idea body weight is considered morbidly obese. (The BMI or body mass index is a better indicator of obesity, but not as easy to measure.)

So the average cat should weigh in at seven pounds. Up to 8.4 pounds would be overweight or fat. Just under 10 pounds would be obese and up to 14 pounds would be mildly obese. Weighing in at 17 pounds meant Huxley was morbidly obese.

Being obese doesn't just mean you have to use more effort to move. It increases the chances of heart disease, type 2 diabetes, breathing disorders during sleep, some cancers and arthritis.

And for all the fad diets for humans, obesity is basically a combination of too many calories in and too little physical activity. There are some genetic issues and endocrine problems, but mostly too much in and too little out.

For humans, this is tough. We have social eating, comfort eating, convenience eating and poor food choices. Pets don't have to make a decision at the refrigerator or drive through. (While I personally weigh in at or sometimes just very near the obese range, my Labrador Retriever is lean.)

For Huxley we tried a Slim Cat®. This is a ball that allows food to be dispensed when the ball is rolled. It requires cats to get more exercise in order to eat. Unfortunately, Huxley (who was mad at me for giving her a pill) refused to have anything to do with something I gave her.

We then tried a diet. Huxley had a six-inch-wide bowl that was about three-inches deep. When I first saw the bowl, it never had less than an inch of food in it. Her owners started measuring her food and allowing the bottom of the bowl to appear. This can be dangerous, because many cats insist on eating at four or so in the morning and will do whatever it takes to get you to feed them. Pouncing on your belly, sitting on your face or scratching you are all fair game to a hungry cat. Feeding the same amount, but just before bedtime can help this.

Also, an obese cat should not be starved. Mobilized fat used for energy will damage the liver and cause Fatty Liver Syndrome. Without extensive treatment, cats with Fatty Liver Syndrome die.

Huxley is responding. She is no longer morbidly obese. She must be feeling better because she plays more. I often try our new toys on Huxley. Of course, she still hasn't forgiven me for the pill episode, but she does play with her gifts when I am not there and the extra exercise helps even more pounds come off.

Less calories in and more exercise is the key.

If only it was as easy for humans.

It's Not Just Puppies and Kittens

So, How Much Should Huxley Weigh?

My friends are responsible pet owners. They care about their cat and this would seem like a reasonable question. Substitute different names and this is perhaps the most common question I get asked. Unfortunately it is also one of the most difficult, if not impossible, questions to answer.

The number on the scale or weight has to do with many things. Health is probably the first. A couple of weeks ago, I had the stomach virus going around. Between 8:00 p.m. and the next morning, I lost more than 5 pounds. If I had felt better, I could have liked losing five pounds. Unfortunately, emptying my gastrointestinal tract from both ends doesn't do a thing for the fact that I am overweight.

Dehydration can be a powerful weight reducer on the scale. Unfortunately, fluid and electrolyte loss is a very dangerous way to lose weight. And it is pointless, the weight comes back as soon as you start drinking and eating what you should.

Mild dehydration is difficult to detect. When laboratory beagles were dehydrated 10% by weight, there were no clinical signs. I'm pretty sure if I lost 15-20 pounds by dehydration, I would feel quite sick, but these dogs did not. If the same holds true for Huxley, she could drop almost two pounds and still look okay, but she still would be morbidly obese.

Muscle is another thing that adds pounds. A pound of muscle is more compact than a pound of fat. On a human, a liter of fat will be 900 grams or 1.98 pounds. A liter of muscle would weigh 1060 grams. Another way to look at it, would be that a liter of muscle requires 15% less room than a pound of fat. So would I love to have another 10 to 20 pounds of muscle? Yes, I would. Ten to 20 pounds of extra fat? No thank you. Been there, done that and extra fat is very difficult for humans to get rid of.

So, a pit bull is allowed to weigh in more than a husky. If Huxley hunted for a living, Huxley could weigh a little more. Of course, if Huxley had to hunt for a living, she would be a lot thinner. At Huxley's current body composition, I am quite sure most of the critters running for their lives would succeed.

It's Not Just Puppies and Kittens

(You have heard the joke about the man who got on his beagle for not running fast enough to catch the rabbit? The beagle replied he "was just running for his supper, the rabbit was running for his life.")

Not only is muscle more compact, it also requires more energy to maintain. More energy out means more fat is used for metabolism and more real fat weight loss. That is why many of my patients are being prescribed a walk several times a week. The exercise itself helps with weight loss, but the muscle mass that is increased uses more energy and helps with weight loss even when not exercising. Of course, if you want to start, a walk benefits owners also.

Bone structure is another component of weight on the scale. A greyhound or whippet will have a lot finer bones than a cocker spaniel or a bulldog. On a side note, I have tried to point out to my MD that I have big bones. Although this may be true, he still writes unpleasant things about my weight in my chart and we have a 'discussion' about it. Anyway, even after two articles about her, Huxley still has a small head and therefore small bones.

So how do I know Huxley was morbidly obese? The same way we know a human is. We look at them. I don't know of any kids who ask how much another kid weighs before they start calling them "Tubby" or "Lardbutt." The same is true of pets.

The ideal pet body should have a waist when seen from the top. It should have an abdominal tuck when viewed from the side. And you should be able to see the last few ribs on a short haired dog. (Normal cats never have short enough fur to see ribs.) Dogs should not look like a tube or exploded tube. Cats should not have a paunch. Actually neither should humans.

So, how much should Huxley weigh?
Less.
A lot less.
That is the most accurate answer.

It's Not Just Puppies and Kittens

Ew! Don't Kiss Me!

Around here, it is not morning breath that is the problem but dog breath. Halitosis is the word for bad breath. When you smell it, it means there is a problem, but bad doggie breath is just the tip of the iceberg. Gum disease is an infection. It results from soft dental plaque building up on the teeth surfaces. Plaque containing bacteria irritate the gums which can lead to infection of the bone around the teeth.

Tartar is the hard stuff that is made up of plaque and deposited calcium compounds. Tartar can form in just a few days and then makes a rough surface which is a better place for more plaque to accumulate.

As the gums become more irritated, they bleed and hurt. In later stages, pets may lose their appetite or drop food as they try to eat.

If the problem were just with the teeth, we would pull all the teeth and feed them canned food. But periodontal disease affects more than just the teeth.

The roots can become so severely infected that the teeth are loose and fall out. Meanwhile the bacteria surrounding the roots get into the irritated gums and bones and then into the blood stream. This bacteria then likes to grow and then damages the liver, heart and kidneys. These infections can cut the life span of a pet by 20-30%.

I don't know about you, but house breaking is hard enough; I don't want to do it again any sooner than I have to. Uh, I mean, I love my pets dearly and want them around as long as possible. Okay, so both reasons are why I do dental care in my petkids.

Prevention is the key to dental disease management. If the tooth's surfaces are kept clean, the gums will stay healthy. This is usually obtained by daily oral cleaning. The Veterinary Oral Health Council (VOHC ®) says the gold standard is daily brushing. While daily brushing is ideal, three times a week is pretty good. Anything less than once a week, probably isn't helping a lot. The best way to start is to hold their mouth shut and go along the front and each side of the mouth. The tartar will not build up and move to the inside until it is bad on the outside. A treat afterward is a great motivator to pets holding still.

Daily chewing does help. At Guardian Animal, we recommend the rawhide bones or flat chips. It is important to buy US made rawhide. If possible, it should also say it is salmonella or bacteria free (both mean the same thing). Even then, I still would not recommend anyone chewing on a rawhide after the dog chewed it and it has been laying around. Chopped and pressed rawhide can include formaldehyde which is quite toxic.

There are dog and cat treats and foods proven to decrease tartar and plaque. Your veterinarian can help you with some.

But sometimes things just get out of control. To be honest, my lifestyle does not allow time to brush Ranger's teeth daily. I do well with the treats, food and sealants, but do not keep up with daily brushing. So every so often, Ranger comes in to Guardian Animal Medical Center and gets blood work done, anesthesia and then he gets his teeth cleaned and sealant applied. Even though I do brush my teeth daily, I still have to go and get my teeth professionally cleaned. I don't mind the dentist and even like mine, but Ranger seems to enjoy it more than I, perhaps because he gets canned food after he wakes up. But even if I brushed his teeth every day, he would need periodic professional dental scaling in addition to ongoing plaque control.

The sealant does help between cleanings. It is best first applied in the hospital and then applied weekly. It forms a coating on the teeth that makes it hard for bacteria to attach.

Oh, by the way, and it is not just dogs with bad breath. Cats get plaque, tartar and periodontal disease and need care also, but I have yet to get a kiss on the mouth from a cat.

It's Not Just Puppies and Kittens

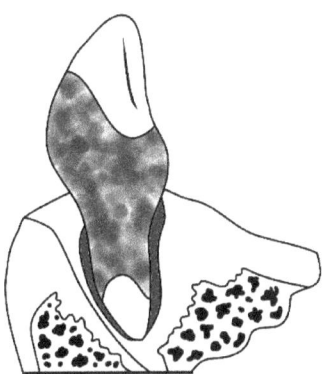

It's Not Just Puppies and Kittens

Thunder! Lightning! Fear!

Ziggy used to hate storms. This little schnauzer came to live with us when she was about 10 and had learned storm anxiety at her previous house. Every time the weather was bad or another storm was going through, Ziggy would be terrified and under the bed.

Some dogs are even worse. One author describes this anxiety as the three P's: panting, pacing and pooping. (By the way, I think cats just hide behind the sofa and we don't see their anxiety.)

Is your pet this way? Do you wonder if there is any way to help? While thunderstorm anxiety may seem helpless, just about anything can be helped. And sometimes help is not extensive or expensive.

The best way to deal with a storm phobia is to not let it happen in the first place. When my daughter was young, I read an article that said the author's father had taken her out on the porch to enjoy thunderstorms when she was a baby. She reported it worked and she did not fear storms, but rather enjoyed them. I guess I was too busy or didn't do enough or start early enough, because M'Kinzy does not like storms as well as I. The same may happen with young animals.

If a dog is fearful of storms, they should not be left outside. Drawing the curtains will help limit the lightening seen. A radio or TV can add noise that helps with the thunder. This will not be a cure; the dog will still see around the curtains and hear over the radio.

If your pet has a storm fear or phobia, you can try to desensitize it. This is done by creating mini "storms" at a level that does not bother the pet and gradually increasing the intensity.

Since pets are much more aware of their surroundings than we are, it can be difficult to recreate the storm. Re-creation usually starts with a CD or tape of a thunderstorm. The "music" should be played as quiet as needed to not cause anxiety. Keep in mind this may be quieter than you can hear it. In some pets, lightening bothers the pet more than the thunder. A strobe light can be used to simulate lightening. Again start at a level that does not bother them. Some dogs, and maybe cats, can sense barometric changes and that is their trigger for anxiety.

Regardless, desensitization takes a while. During this 3-4 week period, the pet should not be exposed to a real storm. Of course, avoiding storms is just not possible in this area right now. That is where medications can help. The new class of anti-anxiety drugs provides more options for treatment. Colmicalm ® and others need to be given for the entire season and can be expensive. A quick and relatively inexpensive solution is a tranquilizer. Tranquilizers do not do anything for the anxiety, but make it to where the pet doesn't care as much about doing anything about the anxiety.

All of these drugs are prescription and can be obtained from your veterinarian. There is also a homeopathic treatment available that is nonprescription, but most of my clients have seen more benefits with the medications.

And Ziggy? Since we had a pack of dogs that were storm non-phobic, she learned from them it was okay. I guess, they did teach the old dog new tricks.

Author's Note: Since this writing, several new supplements and clothing have come out to help with anxiety.

It's Not Just Puppies and Kittens

Hot Dog? Not Cool!

It is summer. It is time to be outdoors. Your pet is family and you want them to be with you when you are doing the outdoor things, but you just have to stop by wherever first. It will only take a moment.

That is a recipe for disaster.

I am always amazed at the sauna that greets me when I open the truck door in the summer. Even with the door opening and the windows down, it is several minutes before it is merely hot.

"But it is not that hot and it will just be a minute."

Nothing is ever "just a minute."

A Stanford University study showed even on comparatively cool days, such as 72 degrees, a car's internal temperature will rocket to 116 degrees within 60 minutes. An 80-degree day becomes 123 degrees inside a parked car in the same hour. **Keeping the windows open a crack hardly slows the rise at all.**

If it is warmer out, the car heats up quicker and to hotter temperature. Even with the windows cracked, outdoor temps in the 90's can result in temperature increases to 115 degrees Fahrenheit in about 15 minutes.

I don't know about you, but I think 115 F is beyond hot.

It's Not Just Puppies and Kittens

The car left in the sun acts like a solar oven. The shortwave radiation of the sun easily travels through the atmosphere and the windows of the car. The air and windows are warmed very little. But this shortwave energy heats the dashboard and seats. A dark dashboard or seat can reach temperatures in the range of 180 to more than 200 degrees F. Then these objects heat the adjacent air by conduction and convection. The sun's rays are also changed to give off longwave radiation which stays in the car and is very effective at warming the air trapped inside a vehicle.

It is not just pets that die in cars. Since 1998, there has been an average of 37 child hyperthermia deaths a year. (These rates have risen, probably due to air bags requiring kids be left in the back seats.) Elders left in cars are a risk also.

Pets, kids and older folks do not handle the heat as well. Dogs only sweat on their paw pads and their noses. They rely on panting to provide the evaporative cooling that we get by sweating all over our bodies. Unfortunately, evaporative cooling requires low humidity; something not found in a closed car.

It's Not Just Puppies and Kittens

Once a dog's internal temperature from heat stress reaches 106 F, there are rapid systemic changes to the liver, kidneys, heart and brain. This requires expert veterinary care. If you find a pet suffering from heat stress or heat stroke, you should pour water on its head and drive with the windows down to your veterinarian immediately. The a/c is not as efficient at cooling the brain (the most important organ) as the water and moving air.

Veterinary care includes evaluation and core cooling which includes IV fluids. Although it would seem like a good idea, ice packs can make things worse. When placed on the extremities they can lead to vasoconstriction which slows the circulation and increases internal temperature.

It is better just to prevent this all together. Use the drive-through at banks, pharmacies and some restaurants. Some stores allow pets. Pet stores often carry some "human" items like candy and snacks. Board your pet for the hour, day or trip. Sometimes a travel kennel in the shade can be a good idea, but in the sun it will still heat up. Don't leave a carrier where it will be bothered by bystanders. If you leave your pet in a carrier, be sure to leave water.

If you see a dog (or child or elder) in a car, don't be afraid to speak up. If you feel uncomfortable calling 911, talk to the store manager, a friend or family member.

I cannot imagine being baked is a pleasant way to die.

No pain, still gain.

Gunner really enjoyed his swimming today. It has been a few sessions and he hasn't enjoyed all of them, but then I didn't really enjoy all of my physical therapy sessions either and I knew why I was hurting.

Veterinary physical therapy has been clinically used in Europe for 15 years, but is just starting to be accepted in the US. Much as in human medicine, we are starting to look at preventing disease instead of waiting to cure it.

Physical therapy must start with a diagnosis and referral by a veterinarian. Starting without this can cause a lot of damage. A certified canine rehabilitation practitioner has been to school to perform physical therapy. These specialists can be found in major metropolitan areas. Veterinary technicians and assistants may perform physical therapy under supervision.

Working together, the veterinarian and physical therapists design a plan for each animal. Neurological conditions tend to improve best with balance and coordination exercises, and muscle building exercises. Surgical repairs and traumatic injuries do better with heat therapy, cryotherapy, cold laser therapy, and massage. Hydrotherapy works for both types of injuries.

Balance exercises strengthen weak muscles. They may include balancing on balls, wobble boards and balance boards. These force the dog to put weight on the injured muscle thereby building muscle in the atrophied area. Coordination exercises force the pet to be more aware of their surroundings. Weaves, figure eights and walking over obstacles build coordination by forcing the dog to shift weight quickly as it turns.

Muscle building is what we usually tend to think of going to the gym for. Treadmill, ramp or step walking uphill and downhill all build muscle and increase flexion of the hip joint. Both standing on two or three legs and getting up from a sit build muscle and can be used after surgery or for hip dysplasia.

Hydro means water and therapy means helping, so hydrotherapy is using water to improve muscle and joint function. Swimming and an underwater treadmill are probably the most effective. Swimming builds more muscles than painful walking would allow. This builds more muscle and endurance without the stress on the joints. The underwater treadmill is the same as land exercise without the stress of full weight on the dog's legs. This can be very beneficial after surgery.

Massage increases the blood flow to the area and relieves muscle spasms. This can help speed up recovery from injuries and surgery.

Thermo (heat) therapy uses heat to decrease stiffness in joints and to increase blood flow. Laser therapy can be used to stimulate healing of surface wounds, pain relief and deep heating of muscles. Cryo (cold) therapy is often used after physical therapy to relieve pain and swelling.

Passive range of motion (PROM) is the repeated flexion and extension of the joint to its limits. This can be practiced at home AFTER being taught by your veterinarian. Stretching too far can cause muscle and tendon damage and pain. (I would bite if you stretched my damaged knee too far.)

And Gunner was headed to recovery, also. He was not fond of walking, even with water, but if his tail was any indication, he really loved today's swimming physical therapy.

I'm sick. Hold the antibiotics.

No, really, I am sick. Parts of my body hurt that I am certain are not recently used muscles. It is difficult to swallow, my nose is raw and it is takes effort to breathe. I also know I am sick, because I went to the doctor. But I fully agree with his decision to not put me on antibiotics.

Some doctors will use antibiotics to treat colds, coughs, runny noses or the flu. But these upper respiratory infections are viruses. There is no reason to treat them with antibiotics. The drugs only kill bacteria and are of no value in treating viral infections. The same is true of some veterinarians treating viral infections with antibiotics. Now, there are some viral infections (like parvo virus) that so throughly trash the immune system that antibiotics for secondary infections are needed, but this is a special use.

The second question, your health care provider should answer before dispensing antibiotics: "Is it the right antibiotic?" I see quite a few exotic pets and I am amazed how often the bird or lizard has been put on totally useless antibiotics that may even toxic in that species . Likewise a drug not cleared through the kidneys would be worthless for a urinary bladder infection.

Antibiotics should never be given less often or for less time. If they are not given for the right reason or the right dose, drug resistance occurs. Think about the population that is left behind every time you kill some. These are the more resistant of the batch. (The easy-to-kill ones died early.) Now with more food, space and time, the remaining bacteria will reproduce. So if a dose schedule was stopped early, the remaining bacteria would repopulate AND be resistant. Likewise with skipped doses.

An example: an infection starts with a million bacteria. It is treated with an inappropriate antibiotic that only kills 40% of the bacteria and the bacterial population doubles every 12 hours (not uncommon by the way). So at the end of the first of two treatments for the day, we have killed 400,000 bacteria. The remaining 600,000 bacteria divide and reproduce and we have more than a million somewhat resistant bacteria. Each dose only kills up to 40%, then those remaining reproduce, so each dose creates more and more resistant infections. At the end of five days, you would have over a million bacteria that are in the top ½ percent of resistance.

Even without resistance or super bugs being produced, there are still significant side effects to antibiotics. Dog bites are a bacterial infection hazard. Since the hands get relatively little blood supply, dog and cat bites to the hands are wonderful uses of antibiotics. But the resultant diarrhea, nausea and stomach pain make me really careful about getting bitten.

Sometimes there are alternatives to antibiotics. Raw cranberry juice has an inhibiting factor that prevents some bacteria from attaching to cell surfaces. This is why it is used in bladder infections. Still best to ask, because your doctor may be able to tell you that pasteurized cranberry is ineffective.

Your doctor and veterinarian should be willing to discuss these things with you, but you should also trust them and take or give the medication as prescribed. If you are not going to give it, say so in the exam room so another plan can be developed. If something happens when you start the medication, call. If you truly do not trust them, you should find another doctor.

Antibiotics save lives and they are important medical tools, in the right situations. My situation, however, looks viral. Red throat, no blisters or pus, ears clear and clear chest sounds point toward a virus. I am told to rest and drink plenty of fluids. Mountain Dew, chicken noodle soup and some bronchodilators and I do feel better. I like and trust my MD, because he is smart enough to know I don't need anything else.

It's Not Just Puppies and Kittens

It's Not Just Puppies and Kittens

Yapper is having puppies!

Excitement buzzes through the Center. Yapper has had the first of six puppies. She is in for protective custody, because she has valuable puppies and the new owner has not delivered puppies before. Besides, it is cold outside.

Yapper was bred 60 and 62 days ago. Since she should have puppies 62 days after breeding, the puppies are due either today or in two days. When I came in this morning, I looked at her and "knew" she would deliver today. There are three stages of labor, and something told me she was in stage I labor. Normally, stage I labor has behavioral changes like anxiety or restlessness. There may be panting, anorexia, vomiting and shivering. Yapper was not doing any of these things, but neither did she greet me on my morning rounds. Stage I labor lasts for 6 - 12 hours and uterine contractions are not detectable externally, but the cervix dilates completely.

Stage II labor is the active portion of labor. The fetus is expelled to become a puppy. Visible uterine contractions and straining should deliver a puppy within 1-2 hours of the onset of stage II labor. After a puppy is delivered, mom may have a resting period. Resting can last up to four hours, but active straining should result in another puppy in five to 30 minutes. Two pups can be delivered in rapid succession, especially with a large litter. (If there is more than four hours between puppies or active straining for more than 30 to 60 minutes, there may be a problem.)

Stage III labor is the expulsion of the placenta. This usually is five to 15 minutes after the puppy comes out. (Neither puppies nor placentas should be pulled.) Multiple placentas may follow the delivery of pups if they are whelped in a short period of time. The greenish fluid is normal. It is called lochia and is associated with placental separation.

But Yapper is having a problem. The second puppy's sac is out for 30 minutes without a puppy. As long as the sac is unbroken, the puppy is still getting nutrition from mom and we have time. But this is officially a dystocia or difficult birth. (And here I thought they all were!) Uterine inertia is when the uterus doesn't contract anymore. If it is because of a blockage or too small pelvic canal, surgery is the only option. In Yapper's case we took X-rays yesterday and documented six puppies and a large enough pelvic canal. But inertia can be caused by only having one puppy, too many puppies stretching the uterus, stress/anxiety or metabolic problems.

Low calcium is a common problem due to improper diet. Yapper eats a high quality proper diet, so in her case, the low calcium was due to her small size and the number and size of the puppies. She got some calcium/phosphorus injections and later some oxytocin to stimulate contractions. That got us puppy number two and before that one was out of the sac, puppy number three arrived. But after more injections and more waiting, Tyler and I are waiting and still no puppies. Yapper seems happy in her resting phase. If everything is normal, we wait. I saw one cat go for two days between kittens.

No matter how long I do this job, I think I will always revere the miracle of birth. Tonight I share that joy with a young man starting toward this career. He will remember this night forever. I know, because I still remember my first time I helped bring a new life into the world. By the way, Yapper delivered all six of her puppies, with only a little extra help.

Death and Dying

I guess it was inevitable. I celebrated life last week. This week was, well, best described as a peak sympathy card week. It didn't help that a close friend's mother was also at her life's end.

As a veterinarian, I understand death is a part of the cycle of life and it is part of my job to help people through the grieving process. That doesn't mean it is easy. With the patients that died or were euthanized this week and a couple of really close calls, I was struck by the similarities and the differences of death.

In human medicine, there is a team that delivers bad news and describes the process of dying. Clear, direct communication was delivered professionally by trained hospice members. There is usually time, measured in days or longer, for the family to adjust. For an animal, there is generally not as much time. The process may only be seconds, minutes or hours. Animal treatment outcomes must be weighed against costs and potential suffering. Immediate decisions must often be made not only to save lives, but also because there is always the option to treat with euthanasia.

But hospice was great. Their care was not only for the person, but also for the family. Without adding false hope, the patient was as comfortable as possible. Hospice did many care items so they did not have to be done by the family. This was an important part of care.

Hospice also provided for spiritual desires with a counselor. (Personally, I think the family had this covered, but was told it did help.) This is difficult or impossible to provide in veterinary medicine.

Something the family was encouraged to do, but perhaps we do not do enough in veterinary medicine, is to give permission to let the loved one "let go" without making him/her feel guilty. This can be difficult. But a dying being will try to hold on, even with prolonged discomfort, if they feel they are needed. From a hospice brochure: "Therefore, your ability to release the dying person from this concern and give him/her assurance that it is alright to let go whenever he/she is ready is one of the greatest gifts you have to give your loved one at this time."

Saying good-bye is probably the most difficult thing I have ever done. It is described as "your final gift of love to your loved one." Difficult, but it achieves closure and makes the final release possible. Tears are a normal and natural part of saying good-bye. They happen even to staff at a veterinary hospital and do not need to be hidden. Tears express love and help you to start the grieving process and let go. Recommended final words may include "I love you" "Please forgive me," "I forgive you," and "Thank you for...."

One more thing that is much different is the amount of support society gives. Family friends and relatives pay respects. This can be at the home, a visitation time and/or a service. Sorrow and tears are expected, not just accepted. Afterward there is an accepted mourning period. Friends and relatives help until grief eases and the comfort of new routines is established.

The processes of grieving are the same for any family member. Different people will have different levels of attachment to each. And death can be a blessing to some people. Grieving a human loss has some distinct advantages for those 'going on' but from whatever angle you look at it, the process of dying and resultant grieving is going to ruin more than just one day.

What is Toxic?

We had a client ask if our snow melt was nontoxic or if they needed to wash their pet's feet. The staff didn't want to give a wrong answer and came and asked me to make sure.

The answer to the second part is easy, yes. The first answer is a little complex.

From www.en.wiktionary.org/wiki/toxic, toxic is defined as having a chemical nature harmful to health or lethal if consumed or otherwise entering into the body in sufficient quantities.

Well, isn't that everything? Table salt (found in our ice melt) toxicity "can result when excessive quantities of salt are ingested and intake of potable water is limited. Salt toxicity is unlikely to occur as long as salt-regulating mechanisms are intact and fresh drinking water is available. It has been reported in virtually all species of animals all over the world. In the USA, it is more common in swine (the most sensitive species), cattle, and poultry. Sheep are relatively resistant. The acute oral lethal dose of salt is 2.2 g/kg in swine and 6.0 g/kg in sheep."*

So salt toxicity is directly related to water consumption. The most sensitive species, pigs, have salt poisoning with .25% salt in their feed if their water intake is limited. But with plenty of fresh water, 13% salt in feed may not produce symptoms. (Don't forget frozen waterers can limit water supplies.)

I truly enjoy another toxic substance. To overcome some of the negativity of some of my facebook "friends," I started listing something I was grateful for every day of the month of November. Coffee was mentioned in five of those days. However, coffee is toxic. Excess coffee can cause restlessness, hyperactivity and vomiting. Even more can lead to panting, weakness, gait abnormalities, increased heart rate, muscle tremors and convulsions in both humans and animals.

Although a person would have to have 150 espressos to get to this point, don't forget pets are smaller and other sources of caffeine include caffeine pills, coffee beans and coffee, large amounts of tea, and chocolate.

(Chocolate has a double whammy of toxins with both caffeine and theobromine.)

Everyone knows if you drink too much alcohol, it can be toxic or even fatal. But if you drink way too much water, the same thing can happen. (So don't drink far in excess of 1-2gallons of water a day.)

But back to ice melts, the first website I pulled up did not list the exact ingredients. (Danger! Danger! Will Robinson!) It did say it had glycols. Hmm, like ethylene glycol the ingredient in antifreeze toxicity? That doesn't sound good.

From http://www.ossian.com, who do nothing but make ice melting products, "the most common, and often sole ingredient in ice melters labeled "Pet Safe," is Urea (sometimes listed as Carbonyl Diamide or Carbamide Resin)." Urea is a chemical commonly used in fertilizers. "Although Urea won't harm your pet's paws, it also won't melt your ice. An over application of Urea, which is inevitable as you struggle to melt ice with it, can have damaging effects to the surrounding vegetation and contamination to water runoff." It is also very expensive. A bag of sand or gravel will do the same thing and be a lot cheaper, even if it doesn't have a pet safe label.

(But from a urea toxicity site: urea's LD50 is listed as 3g/kg which seems to be about the same as salt.)

Ossian company goes on to say most ice melters sold (except for calcium or magnesium chlorides,) if used according to their label instructions will not harm pets with normal contact. "You must however, always be aware of your pets, their health and their behavior. The safest thing you can do is avoid the use of ice melting chemicals altogether. If you must use a chemical be aware of your pet at all times and immediately remove the slush and dissolved product after it has done its work. Taking a moment to wipe off your pet's paws will also be a big help. Your pet will thank you."

It's Not Just Puppies and Kittens

I just put a puppy to sleep

    I just put a puppy to sleep. Forever. Never to wake up again. Not because he was sick. Not because he was hurt. Just because there are too many puppies in the world. He was the last in his litter. The rest had been sick and died or were hit by a car and killed. You see, nobody loved or cared about his brothers and sisters either. In a lot of ways, he was the luckiest of the litter. We usually try, and I think all vets try, to see about a home for at least the healthy puppies and kittens, but when there are too many or they are too old or too big, we cannot find them homes. And there are worse things than death. So the puppy without a name sleeps forever now, but how did he come to be? What was his story?

    His story really starts with his grandmother. She was a nice dog and she had a home. She even had some kids to play with. Her human parents decided they wanted her to have a litter "for the children" and she was allowed to breed. And 63 days later she had seven little puppies. She did not have to have a Cesarean section. Unlike a lot of puppy whelpings, this went pretty well. Her owners took the puppies in at three weeks for deworming and at 5-6 weeks for vaccinations. They fed her puppy food during the last trimester and while the puppies were nursing. Therefore all the puppies did well. At 7 to 8 weeks, they started going to new homes. The puppies were cute (ALL puppies are cute), so the first four got homes. The owners thought the other three went to the same home, but they really ended up in a research facility. At least they were not bait dogs for fighting.

    Our puppy's mom was one of the four that got a home, We don't really know what happened to the other three, but only one is still in the original home. But these owners didn't get any more vaccinations or get her spayed. At eight months she was pregnant. The owners didn't want puppies, so they took her out "in the country" and dumped her. She, of course, did not know how to hunt or even protect herself. She had the puppies, there were eight of them. She tried to raise them, but she was always so hungry herself. She continued to lose weight, but the puppies were hungry and then they got sick. Five of the puppies died. That actually made it easier for her to try to feed our puppy and the other two that were still alive. But times were still tough. The abandoned mother decided to try to move the puppies. Unfortunately, she moved them at night along a road. The car couldn't see her or the puppies until it was too late.

The people in the car felt really bad, but there was nothing they could do. They spent twenty minutes catching our puppy to bring him in. But they couldn't keep a puppy. We couldn't keep a puppy. The shelter was full. (The puppy was wild and scared and would have needed a very special home and even still might not have been a good pet.) So, he was humanely, quietly with a few tears from us, put to sleep. Forever. Never to wake up.

This, of course, is a composite fictional story. Had I known of any of these facts as it was happening, I would have tried to prevent it. However, I and I daresay every veterinarian in town, have seen every aspect of this story many times repeated. Think before you decide to have a litter. Exactly what is going to happen to each of those pups. And one more thing: the grandmother to our pup, well, she developed cancer and died early. That, too, could have been prevented by having her fixed before her first heat cycle. So no part of this story has a happy ending. But it could have. Spay or neuter your pet, please. Stop the pain of the nameless puppies and kittens.

Author's Note: This article was written several years ago. But obviously we still need it because yesterday morning, I posted this on Facebook: "Dear Chicken S***, exactly why do you think we would want your sick kittens in a box on our doorstep? Where does that money come from that takes care of the kittens? I didn't see a donation from you, nor do I get money from the government. Your tax money pays the shelter, if you are not happy with them, call your county judge executive. Or did you bother to try? And how long on a cold night were they there? The blanket in the bottom did not stop the bottom of the box from being wet. Don't worry, we took care of them. signed Stressed Staff."

It's Not Just Puppies and Kittens

It's Not Just Puppies and Kittens

A Box by the Front Door

We had a box by the front door today. I saw it on the way to drop M'Kinzy off at school and had that sick feeling I was going to have to do something distasteful. It is not a good way to start out a Monday morning.

I guess people think since we work with and love animals, we will just take all of them. But we cannot.

Veterinary hospitals do not get any funding from the state or any other government to take care of strays or excess offspring. Veterinarians work hard to pay the utilities, mortgage and staff. Personally, I have yet to find the staff member who says "just skip my paycheck this month, Doctor."

Some hospitals do work with clients to adopt out puppies and kittens but it is usually in conjunction with a spay or neuter program.

The pet overpopulation problem is huge. A cat can start having kittens at 4 ½ months of age, and dogs can have puppies at six months of age. Both dogs and cats can have litters every three months--that's 4 times a year!

Here is a math problem for the kids: If one cat had six kittens every three months for five years--and if those kittens have kittens--can you figure out how many cats would be born in total? A hint: the mother cat alone would have 90 kittens and then each of those kittens could have 90 more in a five-year period.

But the cat's kitten's kittens are having kittens, too. In five years, the original cat could be a great, great, great, great, great, great, great, great-grandmother. However, you calculate it, it is a lot of kittens. It might make a great Dr. Suess book, but in real life it is too many kittens.

Neutering your pet helps it live longer and be healthier. The females have less breast cancer and uterine infections. The males have less testicular cancer.

"Fixing" your pet helps their personality also. There is a word for a female dog and it is not very nice. And a cat in heat is NOT a good roommate! They yowl and urinate frequently--sometimes all over the house just to advertise for mates. Males always mark their territory "just in case."

Male and female pets will do just about anything to find a mate. Add a few mating pheremones and they become escape artists. Running free means more injuries from traffic or other pets.

Spaying or neutering does NOT make your pet fat. Too much food and too little exercise make them fat, same as us. The difference is they don't have to make a choice at the refrigerator and don't have a stress lunch on the fly.

According to the ASPCA, getting your pet fixed costs a lot less than the cost of having and caring for a litter. It also beats the cost of treatment when your unneutered pet escapes and gets into fights.

Indeed, stray animals pose a real problem in many parts of the country. They prey on wildlife, cause car accidents, damage the local fauna and frighten children. Spaying and neutering goes a long way to reduce the number of animals on the streets.

An excuse I hear a lot is owners want to have a litter for their children to learn about the miracle of birth. The ASPCA has this to say: "letting your pet produce offspring you have no intention of keeping is not a good lesson for your children--especially when so many unwanted animals end up in shelters. There are tons of books and videos available to teach your children about birth in a more responsible way."

It's Not Just Puppies and Kittens

Every year, millions of cats and dogs of all ages and breeds are euthanized or suffer as strays. Unplanned litters could have been prevented by spaying or neutering.

Nobody who works with animals loves this part of the job, whether it is the shelter workers or the veterinarian and their staff. So it is not good to start off the day with a box on the doorstep that someone doesn't even take the responsibility to take to the shelter. If we take them in, there will just be more and more and more. By the way, I would not want the shelter's job. If you think they should be doing more, contact your county judge executive or work with your local humane society or rescue league.

For me, my days of taking in boxes of puppies or kittens ended the cold February morning I found two puppies frozen to death at our door. Every time I see a box at our door, I think of those two pups. I am certain I think of them more than their owners ever did. Although it has been over a decade, sometimes I still see them in the middle of the night.

So this Monday morning, what did we find? Happily, someone had left us a box of newspapers for the kennels.

SECTION 3: ANIMAL DISEASES

Roxie is Sick. Really Sick.

It started with turning her nose up at her supper, then she just laid around. She has a new home and her owners were concerned, but it was not until she vomited that they called. When they described the symptoms, we got her right in. The test confirmed Roxie has parvo virus.

Parvo virus is a dangerous viral disease. It affects puppies and dogs, the first time they are exposed. Exposure is easy, because it is virtually everywhere that has not been disinfected. The virus is ubiquitous. (Ubiquitous is a wonderful word that means it is everywhere. Or there is nowhere it is not. A word that fits God and parvo virus.)

Roxie caught parvo virus at the shelter. She was a young puppy put in with other puppies. It is not the shelter's fault. Like any daycare that did not require vaccinations, young animals bring diseases and share them before they show any signs. Roxie looked great when she went home and when she came in and got her first vaccinations. Once exposed to the virus, it grows and multiplies for three to 10 days before causing any of the signs we see.

Puppies and adolescent dogs catch parvo most often. Like humans and chickenpox, you get it the first time you are susceptible and exposed. Since it is everywhere, even tracked in from sidewalks to houses, exposure is common. Most puppies get some protection from their mother. Maternal antibodies are passed in utero and through the mother's milk. These antibodies protect the young puppies, but are not replaced as the puppy grows up. The maternal antibodies are both good and bad. The young puppy needs the protection, but the same maternal antibodies can block the puppy's own longer vaccination antibodies.

In Roxie's case, her body was growing parvo virus by the time we saw her and she got her veterinary vaccination. In other cases, the vaccine may be improperly handled or given on the wrong schedule or be an ineffective vaccine. Whatever the cause, over half of our parvo cases have a history of an over-the-counter vaccine. Extremely few have veterinary vaccinations.

Parvo virus replicates in rapidly dividing cells. This includes the cells lining the intestine and white blood cell production in the bone marrow. In very, very young puppies, it can even include the heart and cause heart failure. The gastrointestinal cells account for the vomiting and diarrhea. The decrease in white blood cells mean the dog is more susceptible to other diseases. Parvo virus is bad, but parvo with distemper is disastrous.

When most people think of parvo virus, they think of the foul smelling bloody diarrhea. Often the diarrhea is so watery it is thought to be urine. And the smell! There are other diseases that can cause that characteristic smell, but anyone who has been around a veterinary hospital will think of parvo when they smell it. The smell has caused many a new employee to turn green.

Vomiting is another typical symptom of the disease. Usually dry heaves, because the dog is not eating. Actually, the first and very occasionally only, symptom includes a period of not eating.

Treatment involves supportive care. The virus will run its course within a couple of weeks. The problem becomes keeping the pup alive until the virus is gone. Supportive care is best in the hospital. IV fluids, electrolytes, antibiotics and drugs to help with vomiting and diarrhea are the core of the treatment. Various other treatments help the immune system. In a hospital with intensive care, 90 percent can recover to go home and do fine. Home treatment is difficult and often fails, often less than one in four or five live without hospitalization.

And Roxie? Roxie is getting the best of the options. She is in the hospital on intensive care and her parents are praying for her. That is important, because as scientifically proven, prayer does help.

Canine Distemper

He was standing in the road. Cars dodging him. Finally, a good Samaritan stopped and picked him up. He was a sweet pup, maybe twelve weeks old or so. He was grateful for the help, but just a little off.

The folks who picked him up were willing to keep him, if he could be fixed. Unfortunately that was not to be. This puppy with no name had canine distemper.

Canine distemper is a highly contagious, serious disease. The virus attacks the respiratory, gastrointestinal and nervous system of dogs, wild canids, raccoons, skunks, ferrets and sea lions. It is extremely dangerous in puppies.

Outbreaks are serious. We have not seen a lot of canine distemper in the past decade. It does occur in the wild population and is a major reason why we do not treat raccoons. Unvaccinated dogs and puppies that come in contact with wild animals or infected dogs are at risk from the airborne virus.

The first sign of distemper infection is often an eye discharge. Later, they can run a fever, have a snotty nose or cough. Infected animals often have lethargy, diminished appetite, vomiting and diarrhea. Later in the course of the disease, the virus can invade the nervous system. This may show up as twitching, seizures, partial or complete paralysis. If the dog does not die in these stages, the footpads and nose may harden. The old-timers used to call this hardpad disease. Even dogs who do not die may have permanent damage to the nervous system. From the AVMA: "Distemper is so serious and the signs so varied that any sick dog should be taken to a veterinarian for an examination and diagnosis."

Veterinarians use the clinical appearance and laboratory tests to diagnose distemper. There is no specific drug to kill the virus in infected dogs. Treatment is mostly to treat the symptoms and prevent secondary problems and infections. Treatment often doesn't work. Any sick dog is a tremendous risk to other dogs and should be kept separated.

Since treatment is not very effective, it is important to vaccinate. From the AVMA: "Vaccination and avoiding contact with infected animals are key elements of canine distemper prevention."

Puppies are very susceptible to infection. Mother's immunity may block initial vaccine protection and a series of vaccinations should be given. Until this series is completed, it is best to avoid any potential sources of infection, like pet stores, dog parks, wild animals, puppy classes, doggy daycare and grooming. Any reputable establishment or training program will reduce exposure risk by requiring vaccinations and health exams and, of course, cleanliness and isolation of sick puppies and dogs.

Adult dogs need to have an up to date vaccine also. A colleague suggested that the lack of adult dog vaccinations may be why we are seeing a resurgence in distemper. Ask your veterinarian about a recommended program for your dog kid.

Mr. Never-to-be-named came in with the characteristic twitching of the mouth and head that is often called chewing gum seizures. Before we could do anything, he went into a full grand mal seizure. Further investigation let us know an entire litter had been euthanized for distemper a few days ago. At animal control's request and in his best interest, this puppy was permanently put to sleep.

Although, I know it was in his best interest, I liked the decade without distemper better. Please, get your dogs vaccinated, before it is too late.

It's Not Just Puppies and Kittens

It's Not Just Puppies and Kittens

Rabies! Oh, No!

(This is, as are most of my articles, an ongoing true story.) I got a frantic message from a distant friend the other night.

"Our sweet dog attacked a possum IN OUR HOUSE tonight. We have a closet that houses all of our electronics components, and Izzy started going CRAZY in front of it. Matthew opened the door to the closet, and she went running in . . . and came out with a possum in her mouth! He is pretty sure she broke its neck. The critter control folks are here now."

This was the start of a nightmare for my friends. Opossums are very resistant to rabies; however, three opossums did test positive for rabies in New York in 2007. And although the risk was slim, my friends now had to worry about the possibility of rabies. As much as they love their dog, they have three young children in the house. (Only once has rabies been cured in a human and the drug-induced long term coma is not a good treatment option for children.) So regardless of their feelings for the dog, the health department was now involved.

"We are beside ourselves about Izzy (the dog). We have been told by her former owner she was fully vaccinated, but we (STUPIDLY!) didn't ever get the paper records. :("

A properly vaccinated pet that is exposed to a rabid or potentially rabid animal will get a booster vaccination and be observed. An unvaccinated animal doesn't have it so easy. Rabies can take months to years to have observable signs. Although they only transmit rabies right before they die, nobody knows when that period will start. Health officials treat the spread of rabies very seriously. By the way, "properly vaccinated" to the health department means by a veterinarian and other trained professionals. There are many precautions veterinarians take to insure our vaccinations are effective.

So, an hour later, I get: "She's gone. Nothing we could do - it's the law . . . I can't even imagine how terrified she is and I am furious with myself . . . "

It's Not Just Puppies and Kittens

Izzy was a rescued dog, but the new owners had her for several months. Animal control carted off the family pet and left in her place three crying kids. Mom and Dad aren't doing too good either. The events will play out as they will and there is nothing my friends can do.

"Yes, she is in quarantine now. We're just waiting for the rabies results to come back, and we're rattling every cage we can to get it done quickly. The family that had her before us has disappeared, and the vet that was supposedly the one that gave the shot says she didn't. It's a gigantic mess."

"Best case is the test comes back negative and they release Izzy. "

If the animal is never exposed to rabies then there is no danger of getting it. But unfortunately critters get in the house and then even indoor pets are at risk as this case shows.

"Worst case is the test comes back positive and they will euthanize her."

There is no negotiation on this part. In a human with known exposure to rabies virus, they should give massive amounts of antiserum infused around the bite and follow up with vaccinations. Even this is not always effective. Nor is the decision easy, although rabies is virtually always fatal, the antiserum has significant side effects and some people react to the human rabies vaccine. In a pet, the risk to humans just isn't worth it. As a society, we do not risk human life for an animal's.

"Medium case (that sure feels pretty bad!) is an "inconclusive" result that will require a 6-month quarantine. We are not talking a lot about that because it would be horrific for Izzy."

This would also be the case if the animal was not available for testing. Quarantine is not necessarily a good option. Many small excitable dogs just will not survive a six-month quarantine in an animal control kennel. And this quarantine is at the owner's expense, which can really add up.

"Our house is a giant emotional pit right now. Will is crying at the drop of a hat and I'm not much better. I'm hoping against hope the results come in tomorrow."

We wait.

They worry.
And think if only...

It's Not Just Puppies and Kittens

Remember Izzy?

When we last left her, she was in quarantine with animal control. She had captured and killed a baby opossum in my friend's house. Since she did not have proof of vaccinations, Izzy was confiscated by animal control. The opossum was tested and was negative for rabies and Izzy was released. Izzy is very lucky! Not only was the opossum negative, but if Izzy had bitten anyone during her stay it would have been really bad. The health department can, if they choose, require an unvaccinated pet that bites someone to be submitted for rabies testing. This is not a benign test! Rabies testing requires a portion of the brain stem. This is obtained by cutting off the head of the pet. Not nice. Not negotiable.

But luckily Izzy did not bite anyone and I got this from my friend:

"Izzy is home" "She's doing well now. When she got home, she was a total mess! I don't think she did any more than catnap while she was "in." Her eyes were bulging and she was completely skittish when anything moved a muscle near her. She seemed completely disoriented and she had lost a couple of pounds (and on a dog that weighs less than 10 pounds that is very significant). She drank two full bowls of water in less than 12 hours. She usually drinks about one a week or so. But, she's almost back to "normal" now - still seems a little tired, and we suspect she may have picked up a flea or two - though we've yet to actually find any. I'm just so glad it is over."

Yes, things are looking up, but just in case, I answered: "You know she may have picked up 'something' while in the kennel. Just be watching and get it treated."

It is not the fault of animal control. Most try to keep things clean and control diseases, but you cannot take a bunch of unvaccinated animals and put them together and not have some diseases transmitted.

Sure enough, a few days later, "And MJ shoots and scores . . . Looks like she may have kennel cough."

Kennel cough or `Bordetella bronchiseptica` is a highly contagious disease. The disease complex causes an inflammation of the upper airways. It often has a harsh barking or honking loud cough that is easily caused by any pressure on the trachea or windpipe. It can be spread by contaminated air or germs on surfaces.

"Went to the vet today, and we decided to just start from scratch. She drew a complete blood panel, we did urine, etc. and we currently have a pharmacy for Izzy on our kitchen counter - strong antibiotics for the suspected kennel cough, cough suppressants for the hacking, and worm medicine - no evidence of them, but the vet wants to be safe given her adventure. The blood panel will hopefully give some clues about whether anything else is going in inside her, vaccinations will be all redone next week (except rabies, of course), and they'll do her dental and check for whether she's spayed (while she's under). And THEN, I hope this whole episode will be behind us . . . "

And I hope it is, but the incubation period for kennel cough is three to five days. The incubation period for parvo virus and distemper can be up to 10 to 14 days. These will be much more serious if Izzy caught them at the shelter.

My friend had been told the vaccinations were up to date. They were not and the emotional toll has been significant. Not that the money part was cheap either.

"You can add to your article that right now our cost of this little adventure is $400 in Critter Control, $120 to Animal Control, $320 to the vet to treat the issues from Animal Control . . . and counting. <Sigh> . . . "

Prevention is cheaper.

Easier and safer, too.

HGE

"Gracie is in the blue room and the owners said she is pooping blood." (Actually pooping is not the word clients usually use and it is very true!)

Gracie was a wonderful "older" lab. Her owners had taken good care of her and vaccinated her, so we did not have to worry about parvovirus. They also did not feed her people food so pancreatitis and intestinal perforations were much lower on the list.

Blood work and fecal exam soon confirmed Gracie had hemorrhagic-gastroenteritis or HGE. The sentence from <u>The 5-Minute Veterinary Consult</u> is very apropos: "A peracute hemorrhagic enteritis of dogs characterized by a sudden onset of severe bloody diarrhea that is often explosive with vomiting and hypovolemia and a dramatic loss of water and electrolytes into the intestinal lumen."

Okay, take a breath and let's take that in pieces. Acute means sudden onset and peracute means faster than acute. The owners had no warning Gracie was that sick. But if they were not on top of things and brought Gracie right in, she would have died.

Many things cause bloody diarrhea, but there are things about HGE that make it much more serious. In HGE, the intestinal lining loses its integrity. The body then secretes blood, electrolytes and fluid into the gut lumen. The loss of fluid and electrolytes leads to hypovolemia (hypo=too low + vole = fluid volume + mia = condition) which is otherwise known as shock.

Additionally, the healthy lumen keeps bacteria out of the bloodstream. The damaged intestinal wall readily allows for bacteria and toxins to enter the bloodstream leading to septic or endotoxic shock.

Gracie did not have the vomiting or explosive diarrhea that is sometimes seen. Vomiting, anorexia and depression are usually the first signs. Diarrhea comes within 6-12 hours and is concurrent with hypovolemic shock and hemoconcentration. At this point the diarrhea often looks like raspberry jam.

Hemoconcentration is an interesting symptom and to my knowledge only occurs to this degree with this disease. The body secretes so much fluid into the gut lumen (and then poops out that fluid) that the body does not have enough fluid for the red blood cells to move around. The blood then starts to sludge and is no longer able to move through the blood stream. This hemoconcentration allows for the easy diagnosis of HGE. We take a very small amount of blood and spin it in small tubes. The amount of packed red blood cells is read as a percentage of the total blood volume. Normal is in the 50% range. HGE will be above 60%. Sometimes it will be up to 75%. Gracie's was 62% and we had a diagnosis.

    I am not sure the owners truly understood how she could be so sick so fast, but they did listen and heard how serious HGE can be. They consented to treatment and we immediately started Gracie on IV fluids and antibiotics and hospitalization.

    HGE is a scary disease. It comes about suddenly and is deadly. But properly administered treatment is almost always a success. Within 24 hours she was better, but because she was 12, she did take a couple of extra days in the hospital.

    For diagnosing, treating and saving Gracie's life, I was a hero. For forgetting that she was twelve years old and it might take a couple of extra days that cost more, I was not quite such a hero.

It's Not Just Puppies and Kittens

Pyometria

Madeline was just a little "off" and had some diarrhea for the past few days. Not a typical history for pyometria, but that is what she had.

Pyo means pus and metria means uterus and pyometria is what happens when the uterus thinks it is pregnant and fills up with fluid, but it is not pregnant and the fluid gets infected. Then the uterus is just like a several pound abscess that is going to rupture into the abdomen. Although there are hormonal treatments, immediate surgery is the best and often life saving treatment.

But let's back up to when Madeline came in. The owner said Madeline was going in and out a lot and she had noticed a lot of little piles of diarrhea. But other than that, Madeline acted fine. Madeline only eats dog food, so that part was good. When questioned, Madeline's mom said Madeline did have some mucous in the stool. Okay, mucous only comes from the colon so obviously we have colitis. (Col = colon + itis = inflammation or infection, so inflammation or infection of the colon.) The most common cause of colitis is whipworms, even if they don't show up on a fecal exam. Next diagnosis, next patient.

Lucky for Madeline, it did not stop here. Years of experience have taught me well.

Madeline was a new patient to us, so I asked how old she was and when the last time she had been to the vet. The owner said Madeline was eight years old and had never been to the vet.

"Not even to be spayed?"

"No."

Alarms bells are now going off in the back of my head. Dogs over age three have an increased risk of pyometria (and breast cancer).

"When was her last heat cycle?"

"Three or four weeks ago, but she is not pregnant, we watch very closely."

The alarm bells are loud now. Uterine problems can happen at any time, but endometritis happens during heat cycles and pyometria happens

2-8 weeks after a heat cycle. Pyometria is extremely common in the three to six-week period after heat.

"Has she been drinking a lot of water?"

"No, I don't think so. I don't know. A couple pets drink out of the same bowl."

This is an important answer. This owner was brave enough to say she didn't really know. Often owners will think they should know and bluff through an answer. In the case of advanced pyometria, the bacteria will leak through the walls of the uterus and be circulated in the blood stream. This in turn causes kidney damage which can be fatal. The increased bacteria will also cause an increase in the white blood cell count (WBC). This increase is profound. A normal WBC count will be 6-17 thousand. A pyometria will usually be over 30 thousand and I have seen over 100 thousand WBCs.

So, the blood work came back at 20,000 cells, not really high enough to be pyometria and Madeline did have colitis which could explain a 20,000 count. But there was something about this cute little yorkie. Maybe she was just a little too quiet or something. I discussed with the owner that we could take radiographs or x-rays, but I really thought she needed surgery. I explained if I was right, Madeline could die without surgery. If I was wrong, it was a somewhat expensive and risky way to do a spay. In short, I asked an owner who just met me to trust my gut instinct.

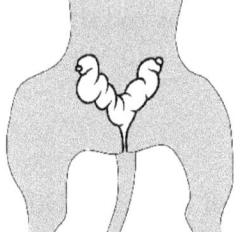

We started Madeline on IV fluids and antibiotics and at surgery found an early pyometria. Because of a few extra questions and time and just a little trust, Madeline is at home and doing well. Oh, and she is being treated for colitis, which probably had nothing to do with the pyometria.

If It Had Been a Snake. . .

    Indy gets to go home today. He is still dripping serum from the two open wounds in his neck, but he is doing so much better. Indy was bad enough that he came in while I was working at the ER last weekend and has been in the hospital for the past six days. For awhile, we didn't really know if Indy was going to make it. Indy's face was almost twice normal size and his neck was also swollen.
    Indy probably got bitten by a poisonous snake. Pit vipers are common in Eastern Kentucky. They are the snakes with triangular heads, fangs and heat-sensing pits. In the U.S., pit vipers include copperheads, water moccasins and rattlesnakes.
    Indy and his brother probably attacked the snake. (If you leave a snake alone, it will usually leave you alone.) Attacking the snake is why most snake bites occur on the pet's head or neck. The snake can inject a little, a lot of venom or no venom at all. The seriousness of the envenomation depends on the location of the bite, number of bites, how still the pet was after the bite (movement spreads the venom), the time of year and the volume of venom present in the snake. By the way, the amount of venom is not related to the size of the snake (even baby snakes have venom) and a bite in the chest area is the most dangerous.
    Venom is dangerous. Locally, it causes tissue damage and death. Systemically, it can cause heart problems, nervous system problems or disrupt the clotting system so the pet bleeds out. Most of the signs are apparent very rapidly, but kidney damage may not show up for three days.
    Sometimes the small puncture wounds are visible. Remember there can be multiple bites. Usually there is bleeding, bruising, immediate and very painful swelling at the bite site and then the tissue dies. It may be hours later, that the severe systemic effects show up. These include shock, lethargy, weakness, muscle tremors, nausea, vomiting and neurological signs.
    Indy's parents didn't know it was a snake bite, and to be honest, we cannot prove it was. But if you can identify the snake, that is good. Be

careful, because even dead snakes can bite. If you do know it is a snake bite, restrict movement of the pet as much as possible. Do NOT cut the wound or try to aspirate the venom. Likewise, ice and/or a tourniquet is a bad first aid idea. You need professional veterinary care.

Your vet will clip and clean the wound and the area around it. IV fluids help to prevent shock and some of the bad-news systemic effects. Sometimes oxygen is necessary. Antihistamines and other drugs are used for the reaction. Antibiotics prevent secondary infections. Pain medication is needed, but NSAIDs are contraindicated in the early phase. Antivenom may be given, but usually not for the snakes in this area. Laboratory tests check for bleeding problems, organ damage and are repeated. Sometimes the pet needs a blood transfusion. Even if it looks like everything is okay, the pet should be observed for at least 12 hours.

If treated with IV fluids, drugs and care, most animals survive a pit viper bite. Even so they can be quite serious. Indy has been touch and go for most of the week. Indy is very lucky his parents brought him right in and that we do not have the Mojave rattlesnake in our area, because the mortality from those bites can be 35%.

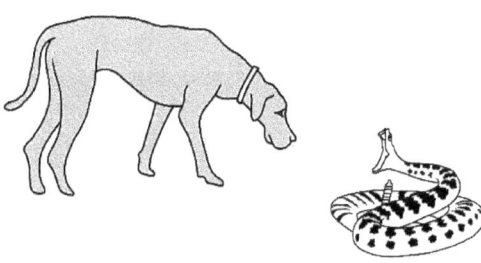

What Was That?

Gracie Sue cried out at 2:00 a.m., stiffened up in bed, and then wouldn't walk on her left front leg for the next couple of hours. The owners were convinced she had hurt herself, maybe even broken her back.

I wasn't there and I didn't see it, but I think Gracie Sue had a seizure. Gracie Sue's seizure may not have been the typical Grand Mal seizure, but her owner's story is. Owners usually see the seizure and by the time the dog is presented to the vet, it is back to normal. (Yes, cats can have seizures, but they are different and cats usually go behind the sofa and we don't see them.)

Of course, you do need to make sure it is a seizure. Some dogs dream deeply and violently, but when a dog is dreaming, they will have rapid eye movement or be in REM sleep. Sometimes heart events or syncope will mimic a seizure also. A true seizure will have a 'pre' period where the dog may seem anxious or find you or a place to hide. This is followed by the actual seizure or period of convulsions. It is possible to have a seizure without convulsions. The mild seizure may not even lose consciousness. There will always be an altered mentation or demeanor, incoordination and slight to significant muscle movement. After the seizure, there will be a period of disorientation. The dog may be blind, deaf or act drunk. This post period can last a few minutes to several days, but usually lasts a few hours.

Primary seizures, or epilepsy, usually first occur when the dog is between six months and five years. Seizures that first happen earlier than six months or later in life are more likely to be caused by either a toxin or intracranial lesion.

A toxin can either be from internal waste products or an organ system failing, usually in old age, like the kidneys or the liver, or a glucose/blood sugar problem like too much insulin or a hypoglycemic puppy. Another form of a toxin would be something eaten like strychnine poison. Intracranial things would include trauma or a tumor. Our female yellow lab had a seizure at age 10; it turned out Maggie had a brain tumor. By the way, with chemotherapy, she lived another two years of happy life.

Although a single seizure rarely lasts more than two minutes (it only seems like forever) and is not life threatening, you should always take your dog into the veterinarian after a seizure. After the first seizure, your dog should get a good physical exam and blood work. You also should start a seizure log. This is not a calendar, because you will often need to keep it for several years. But sometimes you find seizures come only after some event and then you can treat just around that time.

Seizures come either as a single event or as a cluster or group of seizures. Cluster seizures are more dangerous than single seizures. Regardless, the dog needs to be protected from injury during a seizure. Falling off the sofa, deck or landing is going to hurt when they wake up. Seizuring takes a lot of muscle work which generates heat, so seizuring outside on a hot day is also dangerous.

Your veterinarian will help you decide if your pet needs to go on medication now, later or never. The goal of seizure therapy is to have one or fewer seizures every 6-8 weeks. Obviously, if the dog only seizures once every two or three years, daily medication is going to be of questionable benefit.

When you start medication, your dog needs to be on medication for life. Starting and stopping medication is not good and may make seizures worse and harder to control. Most dogs are easily controlled on some relatively inexpensive narcotic pills. However, the younger the dog is when it starts seizuring, the worse the prognosis is and some dogs may not be able to be controlled. Hard-to-control dogs may be given potassium bromide alone or in combination with the narcotic. Some drugs will lower the seizure threshold and allow seizure to show up. Therefore, it is a good idea to always remind your veterinarian that your dog seizures if they are going to give medications. Estrogen also lowers the seizure threshold so you should spay or neuter both to decrease the estrogen and because there may be a genetic aspect which means the puppies would be likely to seizure. You cannot use human medicines because they are broken down in the liver and are relatively useless.

Once your dog starts on seizure medicines, you will need to schedule them for follow up blood work to monitor the blood level of the medicine to adjust the dosage. The longer the dog is on medication, the better the liver gets at getting rid of the medication. This means the dose needs to be adjusted every so often.

And Gracie Sue? She had no pain on palpation of any area of her body. Her range of motion, or ROM, of all of her joints was much better and much less painful than mine. (Her blood work was also better than mine.) Her owners watched a short film on seizures and started a seizure log. If this happens again, her owners will look at her eyes to see if she is dreaming.

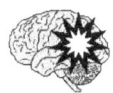

We will see about medicine in the future.

I Touched Her Heart

I love my job. Usually. Most of the time. Not always. Okay, so I like to help people. I like to fix things. I like to prevent things and occasionally be a hero.

I really don't like to give people bad news. Not that I don't, but it is not one of the perks of my job. Bad news can ruin my day also. A couple of weeks ago was one of those days. An owner brought in a new puppy. She was cute with a great personality, but on her physical exam, I heard a murmur. My heart skipped a few beats. I listened carefully to be sure, but it was there. A continuous murmur that sounded like machinery.

Murmurs happen when there is turbulence, but one that happens at all times in the beating cycle almost always means there is either a ventricular septal defect (hole inside the heart) or a Patent Ductus Arteriosus or PDA. Of the two, a PDA is much more common and easier to fix.

The Ductus Arteriosus is the vessel that shunts blood from the lungs back to the body while the animal is in the uterus. (There isn't much point in sending a lot of blood to the lungs.) When the puppy is born the pressure in the now breathing lungs is supposed to shut off the vessel. But in 6 to 8 cases of 1000 live births, the vessel does not close and remains "patient." This means the heart has to beat much faster to move the same amount of blood. This can lead to respiratory distress, coughing, exercise intolerance and stunted growth. In later stages there can be rear leg weaknesses and blood concentration and blood thickening to the point of clotting. Dogs can die of congestive heart failure, arrhythmias or embolus. In fact, 50-60% die from congestive heart failure within a year.

This is what I had to tell Squirt's owner.

There is a treatment. Surgery is very effective if it is done early. This can be to tie off or ligate the shunt or to put in a Gianturco coil that occludes the ductus. The surgical technique for an uncomplicated case looks easy in the text book. Go in find the shunt, tie it off, re-inflate the lung that was in the way and close the chest.

It's Not Just Puppies and Kittens

Of course, the simple procedure is followed by 27 pages (okay, maybe not quite 27) of everything that can go wrong, including the small animal completely bleeding out in 10 to 20 seconds if you tear the ductus while trying to dissect it away in order to tie it off. Oh, and the heart is beating the entire time, so tearing is a real possibility. And the anesthesiologist has to breathe for the pup the entire time because the chest is open. Then there are all the special tools that are only used for this surgery. In short, this is a specialist surgery.

But Squirt's parents had only had him a day and they did not have money for a specialist. They did not want her to go back to the breeder to be resold. Nor did they want their son to get attached to a pup that would die within a year. When they asked us to take her, my team came together and we did surgery. None of us were in our comfort zones that day. We said a prayer for patience and skill before surgery. Within a couple of hours after surgery, Squirt was up and standing. I did my part well, but could not have pulled off this complex surgery without my staff.

We all felt like heroes that day! But with Squirt doing well, we realized that Squirt needed a home. None of us really needed another pup, so as a surprise, we gave the pup back to the original owners. Both staff and Squirt's family had tears of raw emotion.

Author's Note: Six years later, Beanie AKA Squirt is doing very well. The owners got a second Boston Terrier that they named Wix, after me.

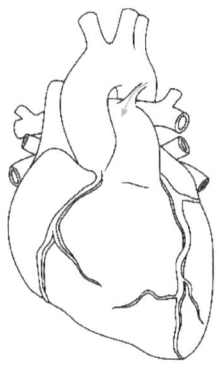

SECTION 4: CATS ARE NOT LITTLE DOGS

Toxoplasmosis

I was sitting down to a high stress meeting yesterday and while we were slowly gathering everyone, five of the ten of us were awkwardly sitting there. To break the ice, a lady announced they were having a baby. A surprise baby.

Congratulations! And I instantly thought back to that decade I was pregnant and then jumped from there to all of the things that can go wrong. (I was NOT a happy pregnant person and the doctor in me wants to prevent disease!)

People started coming into the meeting and I had to go back to protective "mom" mode, but I really intended to mention about cats and toxoplasmosis.

Toxoplasma gondii is a single cell protozoan that requires two separate hosts to reproduce. The Toxoplasma organism uses the both wild and domestic cats as a definatitive host. This means the parasite protozoa can only produce oocysts (protozoan eggs) when they are infecting a cat. These oocysts are passed into the feces in great numbers. An intermediate host, such as a mouse, vole or bunny picks up the oocyst with grass or other things eaten. The oocyst hatches and the protozoan moves from the intestines to the muscles or other tissue. When the cat eats the prey species, the parasite is released into the cat's intestinal tract. In the wall of the intestines, they grow and multiply and produce more oocysts.

The first time a cat is exposed to Toxoplasma, they begin shedding oocysts in three to 10 days. They may continue shedding for 10 to 14 days. These oocysts are very hardy in the environment and can infect intermediate hosts for well over a year. Note they only shed for two weeks, one time and never again under normal circumstances.

This is where people sometimes come in. If you ingest an oocyst, usually from undercooked meat, but sometimes off your hands from the garden or litter boxes, you usually will not know you even have the disease. Some people may have vague flu like signs, like body aches, swollen lymph nodes, headache, fever and fatigue. But normal immune competent people only get it once also.

Of course, if you have HIV or AIDS, have chemotherapy or a recent organ transplant, you are more likely to have signs and symptoms of severe toxoplasmosis infection which could include seizures, poor coordination and confusion. You may even have lung problems similar to tuberculosis.

But babies are the real risk factor. Many times, pregnant women do not have any signs of the disease. (Or they may not recognize it is not just pregnancy. I am certain aliens could have invaded my body and I would not have known the difference.) Even without signs, there is a 30% chance of transmitting the disease to the baby. The earlier an infection happens in pregnancy, the more dangerous it is. But it is more likely to be transmitted later in pregnancy. Early infections can lead to stillbirth or miscarriage. Children that do survive may have seizures, liver/spleen problems, jaundice and severe eye infections. Very few babies have disease signs at birth. Many that are infected at birth do not show signs until they are in their teens or in adulthood. These signs may include hearing loss, mental retardation and serious eye infections and blindness. Obviously, things none of us want for our children.

So, we prevent toxoplasmosis infection by avoiding undercooked meat, anything from where cats have defecated, and wash our hands frequently. Notice, we are not saying that we get rid of the cat. (You keep that cat, but don't get a new kitten.) Which brings me to the only advantage I saw from being pregnant: somebody else gets to clean the litter box! Okay, okay, the other two advantages are that pregnancy eventually ends and we got a great kid.

(From the Mayo Clinic: If you're living with HIV or AIDS or are pregnant or thinking of becoming pregnant, talk to your doctor about being tested. The signs and symptoms of severe toxoplasmosis -- blurred vision, confusion, loss of coordination -- require immediate medical care, particularly if your immune system has been weakened.).

It's Not Just Puppies and Kittens

Feline Infectious Peritonitis

Miss Kitty is sick. She may not make it. In fact, if I am right, she almost assuredly will not. Miss Kitty has Feline Infectious Peritonitis or FIP.

FIP is a virus that starts by growing in the upper respiratory tract and/or the back of the throat. When it is taken up by the white blood cells trying to fight it, the virus moves to blood vein walls and nearby tissues. As it continues to reproduce and multiply, it causes a pyogranulomatous reaction. (Pyo=puss, granul=little grain, oma=tumor/growth, atous=condition of, so a bunch of little puss filled growths.)

This reaction is the typical FIP lesion. It happens throughout the body: in the abdomen, on organs (liver, kidney, intestines), lymph nodes, and inside the intestines; in the lungs, on lung surfaces possibly creating fluid around the lungs; and in the brain and eyes.

If it sounds serious, it can be. FIP happens mostly in kittens three months to three years of age. After three years of age, the disease is extremely rare. (At Guardian Animal Medical Center, we recommend and vaccinate cats up to three years and then drop the vaccine out of the protocol.)

There are two different coronavirus strains, FCoV and FIPV, both of which can cause the whole range of the disease. But just like the human cold, different strains of the virus can have different effects. Many cats have antibodies to FIP, but never have the disease. Some are carriers and transmit it to others and still other cats seem to have thrown off the disease. But if the kitten is one that gets sick, it is bad news.

The disease comes on slowly. Kittens will be depressed with stunted growth. There will be weight loss and a poor hair coat condition. There are two forms of the disease, wet and dry. In the wet form, the body cavities are the targets. Fluid accumulates in the abdomen and around the lungs. In the dry form, the organs themselves are damaged. Sometimes palpation of the abdomen by your veterinarian can reveal the pyogranulomas in the abdomen. Sometimes typical changes can be seen in the retina of the eye. Brain and neurological signs can be just about anything.

Diagnosing the disease can be difficult. A presumptive diagnosis of the wet form assumes the kitten has FIP, if it has a swollen belly and is sick. Dry forms are a lot more difficult to even assume the kitten has FIP. Unlike feline leukemia, feline aids and heartworm disease there is no simple blood test. Remember in testing for the antibodies, many cats have FIP antibodies that do not have FIP disease. Testing for the virus itself is much harder and much more expensive. Not only does the virus have to be in the body fluid sample at the time you take it, the virus has to survive the trip to an often distant specialized veterinary lab. Once the virus gets to the lab, there are even more issues with testing procedures which translates to expensive tests.

So, sometimes we don't diagnosis FIP while the kitten is alive. Sometimes it is only diagnosed with a necropsy after death. Many times the diagnosis requires the trust of your veterinarian, because many sick FIP kittens eventually benefit from euthanasia. In the early stages of FIP, it doesn't hurt to treat the kitten with supportive care. And maybe, sometimes, we treat because, although it doesn't happen often, there are times I would love to be wrong.

Old Skinny Cats

I saw an older cat today. I recommended blood work, but didn't get permission. Still I started thinking about older cat problems.

Older cats get the same things all cats get and several that older humans get. But older cats also get a set of diseases that cause them to lose weight and decline.

This set was called the triad of old cat diseases. Many older cats have one or more of three potentially interrelated diseases. Low potassium, kidney disease and hyperthyroidism makes up the triad.

Hypokalemia or low potassium can be a sign of renal disease or a risk factor for it. Potassium should be absorbed from the food, but poor quality diets or diets that acidify the urine are risk factors. Cats with chronic renal disease are unable to prevent excessive potassium loss. The lost potassium will be taken from the body tissues to maintain the blood levels. Cats with low potassium will often walk with their hocks down, have muscle wasting, weakness or pain.

Low potassium causes problems, but too much potassium causes cardiac arrhythmias and death. So, supplementation should always be under the advice and guidance of your veterinarian.

Chronic renal disease or kidney failure is another of the triad of old cats. Under normal circumstances, the kidneys continue to flush out all toxins out of the blood as long as there is 70% of the kidney still functioning. If there is dehydration or stress or if the damage exceeds 70%, the toxins are not filtered out of the blood and build up and therefore poison the cat.

Cats with chronic kidney disease drink a lot and urinate a dilute urine. They may have muscle wasting and pain. The kidneys also secrete a hormone that tells the bone marrow to produce red blood cells. If the bone marrow does not get the hormone because the kidneys are not working, the red cells are not produced and the cat becomes anemic.

The final disease of the triad is hyperthyroid disease. This is where the thyroid gland produces too much thyroid hormone. Usually the thyroid gland has a tumor, but not always. Thyroxin speeds up the body metabolism. The cat has a ravenous appetite, but cannot maintain weight.

The three diseases often interact. Increased blood flow from hyperthyroid disease will mean the kidneys have more of an opportunity to filter toxins out of the blood. But this increased metabolism puts an increased stress on the heart and blood pressure. Increased blood pressure damages many cells of the body, including the kidney. The increased blood flow can also increase potassium losses.

In short, the triad of cats becomes a juggling act of veterinary medicine. In the very early stages, it can be a very satisfying juggling act, but in the later stages it can be quite frustrating. We probably will do blood work in this cat, but maybe not in time for me to be a hero.

SECTION 5: PARASITES

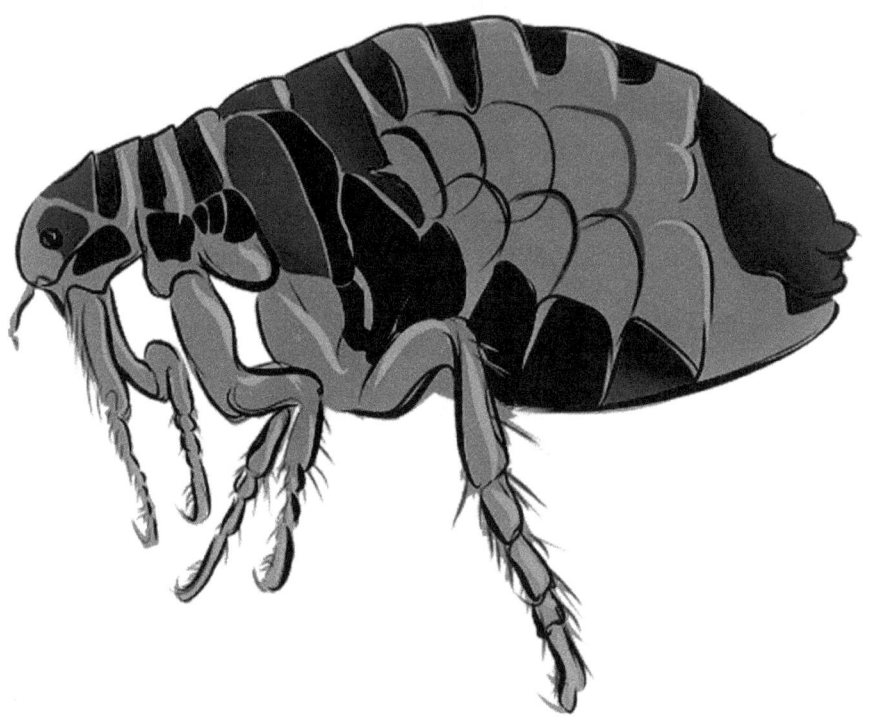

It's Not Just Puppies and Kittens

How Did this Flea Get Here?

It happened again today. A client was in the exam room and her pet STILL had fleas. Indeed I didn't even have to look for them; a flea hopped right on me. Having been through this before, I excused myself to get a piece of packing tape to trap the flea so I could look at it.

(It seems if I just try to look, they always escape, but then fleas are designed to do just that. Fleas are laterally flattened (side to side) so they can run easily between hairs. And they can jump to escape almost being caught.)

But how did the flea get there? The owner was treating with good products on a proper schedule. Let's look at what happened to get that flea. Adult fleas eat, live and breed on their hosts, in this case, a dog. Both males and females live on the pet. Both males and females suck blood from their host. Something I don't think we really want to think about, but the adults then mate on our pets. After mating, the females lay eggs as many as 40 to 50 a day.

These eggs are not sticky like some other insect species and they readily fall off the pet into the environment. Dr. Dryden, who has spent twenty years researching fleas, likens the pet as a flea egg salt shaker. Everywhere the pet is, it shakes out some more fleas into the environment. Wherever the pet spends the most time, will have the most flea eggs.

Eggs start hatching into larvae or flea maggots. The tiny larvae live and grow in the bedding, carpet, floor cracks, baseboards and tile. (They hold onto carpet fibers to resist vacuuming.) The adult fleas feed the larvae by only digesting half of the blood they eat. The other half of the blood meal is in the flea poop which drops off in the same places as the eggs. The flea poop with blood is what the larvae eats. This is commonly called flea dirt. If you streak it on a wet paper towel, it will form red streaks of blood which makes it easy to distinguish from dandruff.

Little larvae molt and become bigger and bigger. After three molts each larva spin a cocoon. Inside the cocoon, the larva metamorphosis into a flea. The flea hangs out in the cocoon until it senses a pet going by. When a suitable host goes by, the flea hatches and jumps to land on the host. The body heat, vibrations, and exhaled CO_2 are used by the flea to find the host. Depending on the temperature, humidity and environment, this can take as little as seven days and as many as 200 days. You can see that even if a product killed all the fleas and continued killing the adult fleas for 30 days, you would still see fleas for several months. Indeed, after a month you would soon have reproducing fleas.

You can tell a baby flea from an adult by its size and color. A newly hatched flea is smaller and black. A mature flea is larger and the females are a brown color. The monthly flea products from your vet are effective but still take 4 to 24 hours to kill fleas. None of our products is a repellent so the fleas will still be attracted to the pet and then killed. Besides, it may be just me, but personally, as much as I love Ranger and Half-A-Cat, I would prefer they have the fleas and not me.

The flea I caught was a little teenager flea. It had just recently hatched out and jumped on the dog. The owner had applied an excellent topical flea medicine and the flea was not happy. In fact, it was going to die before the day was out. Maybe it was hopping on me because it knew I wasn't treated.

My Dog Still Has Fleas

We have heard this statement often this year. Even with very good products, people are still seeing fleas. In fact, I attended a two-hour seminar on this very subject this month. So let's look at some of the issues.

First, many over the counter products are only intended to kill 70% of the fleas. (I don't know about you, but I don't want fewer fleas. I want to be on the path to no fleas.) If you only kill a portion of the fleas and the rest live and reproduce, you will always have quite a few fleas.

But let's examine what happens when you are using one of the excellent monthly products from your veterinarian. All the flea-carrying animals have to be treated. A client yesterday told me her dogs were being treated, but her cat didn't have fleas. Well, that's not the way it works. You may not see fleas on one animal, but they are feeding and causing problems on all of the dogs, cats, rabbits and ferrets. We used to have two brother and sister cocker spaniels. In 17 years, I never saw a flea on Brandy. She was allergic to fleas and smart enough to know that fleas caused her to itch. Brandy would chew until she killed them. Dandy on the other hand, couldn't care less. He was not allergic and not nearly as smart as his sister. You could part the hair on Dandy and the multitude of fleas would go running. If it hadn't been for Dandy, I could have argued we didn't have fleas. Only the parakeet and fish don't need to be treated. (Call about other strange critters. And always check before treating exotics. Some exotic pets react and even die with normal "safe" flea treatments.)

So, step one, treat everyone. Well, not the humans. Fleas can tell the difference between a pet walking by and a human. We don't taste as good so dog and cat fleas are reluctant to be on us. So until they are starving and the house is overrun, don't think seeing no fleas on you means no fleas. When you are treating, it may not just be "your" animals that need treatment. If the neighbor's cat comes and sleeps on your porch where you and your dog watch the sunset, you will not be rid of fleas unless you treat the cat also. Opossums that eat the outdoor cat food or live in your yard can also provide your pets with an ample supply of fleas. In a study in Florida, 100% of the opossums had fleas by the fall.

If you need to treat outside (by the way I am NOT available to help catch and treat the opossums in your area), you do not need to treat the whole yard. Fleas cannot live in the areas that get hot and dry out. So the sunny places don't have fleas. Under trees, bushes and weeds are areas that need to be treated. Don't forget the shaded garage or car port. Treating the sunny, dry yard just adds chemicals to our water supply.

The other "problems" usually have to do with timing. When your pet first gets fleas, chances are that you do not notice right away. If the fleas are there for, say, three weeks before you notice, there are a lot of flea eggs in the house. But eggs aren't the problem we notice. It is possible to have the pet get a few fleas and in the next few weeks the pet grooms them off. The adult fleas are gone without any treatment at all. Unfortunately, the eggs hatch. Depending on the temperature, it may take 6-9 weeks for them to start. The tiny black teenager fleas will be in abundance. So it will look like the monthly product has "failed." After all, there were fleas in the beginning, you treated and they were gone. Next month you treat and no fleas. Third month, when you treat, you will have all of these fleas that have just hatched out. The answer, keep treating. You may need to treat at three-week intervals instead of four especially at the beginning. All of the products from your vet are good. Rotating products may help but probably isn't necessary. Call your vet and ask them to make sure you are doing things right, but stay the course. You may continue to see baby black fleas for months, but they will be killed before they can reproduce. Keep in mind also that not all products have an IGR or Insect Growth Regulator that keeps fleas from hatching.

So, what is really different about this year? We have not had the killing freeze that helps with our outdoor/wildlife fleas. That means there are more fleas in the environment, which in turn means there are more fleas to expose our dogs.

I think our flea resistance is not one of resistance, but yet another effect of global warming.

My dog is Crawling with Fleas!

How many fleas have you seen?

Well, I know she had fleas. I don't actually see any, but she scratches all the time and I saw them a couple of weeks ago before we started treating her.

Ahh, she has a medical condition called a flea allergy or flea allergy dermatitis (FAD), sometimes called atopy. FAD is not really a disease, but a complex. That means that it is not one thing, but a few things that can be treated with similar treatments.

So, technically, your dog or cat doesn't have to have fleas to have a flea allergy. That said, 85% of flea allergy dermatitis is caused by fleas. And one flea bite can cause a pet to itch for two weeks. (If this is a little hard to believe, think about poison ivy.) So, if one flea can keep your pet itchy for weeks, absolute flea control is a must. (My chief editor said we have scratched the surface of flea control over the past two weeks.)

A dog with a flea allergy will have itchy skin with hair loss on the lower back and pelvic region in a Christmas tree pattern starting at the base of the tail. A cat will have itching, 'miliary dermatitis' (like millet seeds under the skin), hair loss in the inguinal region or dermatitis and hair loss like the dog. Add a few fleas and we are more sure of the diagnosis. We assume a tentative diagnosis if the pet gets better when we remove the fleas. But we are not totally certain unless we have all of the signs, results AND a positive allergy skin test for flea saliva.

Flea allergies result in about half of the skin problems in Eastern Kentucky. It definitely can make other diseases such as atopy or food allergy worse. But most dogs and cats are not allergic to fleas. The <u>Ctenocephalides felis</u>, or cat flea, is the most common flea of the dog, cat, ferret and rabbit and is well host-adapted to not cause allergies–in most pets. The fact that we have a lot of flea allergy patients should tell you just how many fleas infestations there are.

It flea bite causes the problem, not the flea or the flea dirt. When the flea bites its host, it secretes a small amount of salvia into the wound.

This acts as a mild anticoagulant to keep the blood flowing. It is this saliva the pet is allergic to. The sensitivity is not just to the spot that was bitten. The released histamine is picked up by the blood and transmitted to the skin which has the highest number of histamine receptors. This means the pet itches all over.

The hypersensitivity or allergy is most likely to form with intermittent flea problems. If the pet has fleas continuously there is less likelihood of a flea allergy developing. Once the allergy forms though, more flea bites mean more allergy symptoms. That means more compulsive biting, chewing, licking especially of the back end.

Medication for your pet can include omega-3 fatty acids, antihistamines, glucocorticoid therapy in either a topical or systemic form. If there is a true atopy, hypo-sensitization (allergy testing and shots) and antihistamines may be necessary for pets that have symptoms year around. There are some new chemotherapy type medications that can be used also. Although common, flea allergy dermatitis is a complex medical condition that is going to need a close relationship with your veterinarian to keep under control.

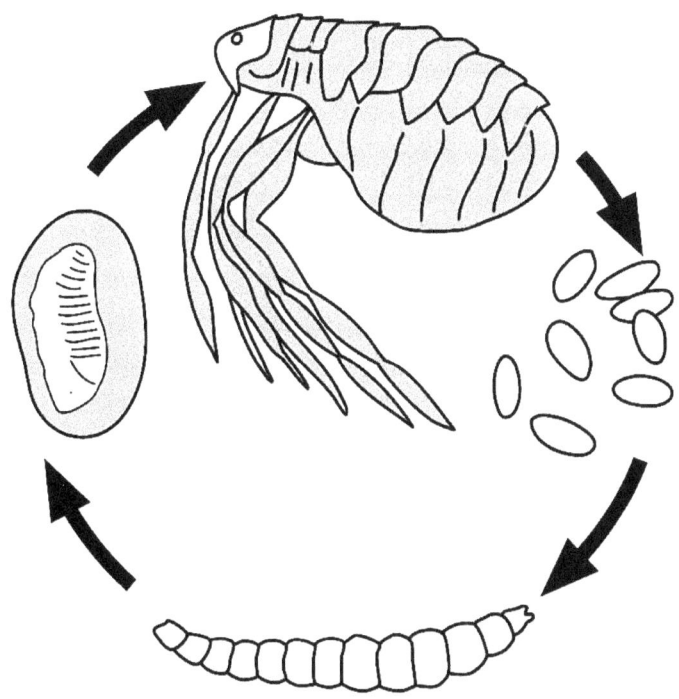

Treatment certainly includes controlling the fleas. Your veterinarian can help you with that, but be very careful with over the counter flea products. Insect Growth Regulators(IGR) help, but you may still be looking at months to rid your house and pet of fleas.

It's Not Just Puppies and Kittens

Now, Mr. Editor, I think we have indeed, scratched the surface of fleas.

SECTION 6: WILDLIFE

It's Not Just Puppies and Kittens

Motherhood in the Animal Kingdom

I never wanted to be a mother. Women died in childbirth. And anyway, I always thought it was too much work.
I had no clue.
But I believe all things happen for a reason. Although I often question Who thought I needed or could raise a child, she is a great kid and I cannot imagine life without her.
Just like humans, there are all kinds of animal mothers in the world. There are insects that carry the eggs or babies around on their backs until they hatch or feed on their own. Earwigs, a type of insect, even take care of their babies.
Lizards and alligators may guard their nests, but have little interest in the young. In fact, if the kids stray too close, they may become a snack.

Birds are a little more maternal. Hawks and owls hunt to bring food back to the nest. But they always feed the oldest first. If there is any left over, the others get fed. Keeping your ducks in a row means to be protectively organized. And birds can be quite protective. How many of us have run afoul of a house wren by getting too close to her nest which is near our house?
But when we think of mothers we usually think of mammals. There are internet photos of the dog nursing kittens or the baby pig. These pictures almost always evoke an "oooohhh, sweet" from human moms.
Elephant mothers coax all the young into the center of the herd for protection. Of course after being pregnant for three years, who would want to start all over? Elephants also form bonds that keep the young adult females in the herd. And speaking of large, although it can't be fun at labor and delivery, hippopotamuses give birth to a calf that is 110 pounds. They deliver underwater and the baby hippo has to swim to get her first breath.
Some mammals take care of the kids, but not the nurturing we would think of. Baby bunnies only nurse once a day. Mom spends the rest of the day foraging or napping. On the other hand, red bats carry their

young with them at all times. The bat pups get so big, the mom sometimes cannot take off in flight. We had a mother red bat at GAMC with twin pups that she refused to abandon but could not fly with.

This nurturing is typical of many moms. But sometimes the same mom can become, well, not so sweet. There is a not very nice name for a female dog.

In stressful situations, mother dogs and hamsters have been known to kill and eat their young. (I know some of us can relate.) In overcrowding stress, mother mice don't actually kill their offspring before starting to eat them.

Sow hogs do occasionally kill their young, but more likely to come after people if they get the piglets. If you hike in a national park in Alaska, you have to go through training to make sure you understand not to go between a bear sow and her babies. (I always wondered if they send the paper you signed to your next of kin if you were a slow learner.)

Maybe that was the Wisdom that gave me this child. Although tempted to kill, eat or at least maim, I can be fiercely protective, which she

does seem to need for a while.

It's Not Just Puppies and Kittens

There is No Daycare in the Wild.

It is spring and the world brings forth young at the time when there are plenty of plants and insects to feed them. Unfortunately, in the wild not all mothers survive and there is not an adoption system in place for young.

This means it is peak season for wildlife rehabilitation.

Orphaned wildlife often finds its way to us or other licensed rehabilitators. Orphans need help until they can be on their own. By the way, the definition of an orphan is the animal (or the child) has lost their parents.

This is not the story for most of the wildlife calls we receive and even some of the wildlife itself that comes in.

Baby birds do not just have all their feathers and fly the first attempt. They are like teenagers and want the car, but don't have the gas money to go very far. These birds are called branchers and will hop from branch to branch, practicing flight, but cannot actually fly. These branchers are often found on the ground. The best thing to do is make a nest; a margarine tub with holes punched in the bottom is good. It is a myth that bird parents will abandon their young after people have handled them. In fact, most birds cannot smell very well at all.

Baby bunnies and fawns are left alone by their mothers for 12 to 24 hours at a time. In case you were wondering, there is no day care in the wild. Babies are left, while the mothers feed to make enough milk to feed them. Eastern cottontails, for instance, power nurse their babies a rich milk once a day. Usually this is about three or four in the morning. (I don't know about you, but that is not my peak rabbit watching time!)

Even does that go back to their fawns twice a day will not return to them if they think there is danger. A human watching definitely qualifies as danger.

Unless they are hurt or threatened, wildlife should be left in the wild. Still sometimes mom is dead and we can see her, a pack of dogs chase a fawn into a swimming pool, or something else that means the young needs to be "saved."

It's Not Just Puppies and Kittens

The Guardian Animal Medical Center staff has most wildlife 'stuff' down to a routine, but bats are different.

And, I have a baby bat. The bat is an orphan; starving, she left her roost and was picked up by humans who brought her in. One of two bats so far this year, she has lived a couple of weeks. Baby bats have to be fed several times a day for several weeks. Many baby bats don't make it in foster care.

We are a licensed rehabilitator, but we receive no funding from either state or federal funds. While we cannot take in all wildlife (and no raccoons, skunks, poisonous snakes or monkeys), we do try to help. We will teach baby bird and rabbit care and take in some others. Raccoons and skunks can carry and transmit rabies without showing any signs. Raccoons also transmit raccoon roundworm that can burrow through the spinal cord and brain of humans and pets. Raccoon distemper is an often fatal, airborne disease transmitted to dogs; something we cannot afford to have in the hospital.

Obviously, a bat is something most people cannot handle at home. Even as a baby there is a risk (although extremely slight) of rabies virus. That means it is safer to have the rehab done by someone who has a rabies vaccine. At our hospital, that is only me. So, I am in three to five times a day to feed the critter. (More on bats later!) My friend says the baby bat is cute. Personally, naked, blind and hairless don't do anything for me. But she is starting to have some personality and is now picking her back leg up to scratch her neck which is kind of cute.

But like all honest evaluations of wildlife rehabilitation success, most do not make it.

But some do. So, I trek in to feed. And try.

Maybe to help this one.

I Have a Bat in My Pocket

There is a book by that name. I have never read it, but it looked interesting and since I am hand raising an orphan baby bat, from time to time, I do have a bat in my pocket.

I am aware not all people think bats are as neat as I do, but they really are amazing creatures.

Bats are endangered. A single act of vandalism can kill millions. They usually only produce one pup a year. Now white nose syndrome, a newly emerging fatal bat disease, is killing bats by the thousands. Several more species may become extinct in the United States and Europe.

There are more than 1,100 different species of bats. Some eat nectar. Famous ones lick blood, but over 70% of all of the bats in the world eat insects. All of the bats in Eastern Kentucky are insectivorous. This means they only eat insects. Many of these small bats can each eat more than 1,000 mosquito sized insects in one hour. One bat. One hour. Bats don't come in ones and they hunt all night. The 20 million Mexican free-tailed bats from Bracken Cave in Texas eat about 200 tons of insects a night. Each night.

Even though they fly, bats are not related to birds. Bats are mammals with fur and they nurse their young. They are the only mammals that truly fly. Others glide, but bats fly.

Bats also echolocate like dolphins and whales. Bats make high frequency calls from their mouths or noses and then listen for echos to bounce back from objects. This means they can fly in complete darkness. Bats can avoid objects, move around obstacles, avoid predators, locate and capture their food all without any light.

Still, bats are not blind. Most see as well as a human. While we are discussing myths, bats do not get entangled in human hair and seldom transmit disease to other animals or humans.

Bats hang upside down in order to use roosting space away from predators in the safe places on ceilings of caves, in trees, and buildings that few other animals can use. Bats have specialized tendons that hold the feet closed when hanging upside down. They must contract muscles in order to release their hold on the ceiling. A bat heart is made slightly differently to pump blood "upside down." Also, the knee caps are rotated completely backwards from ours to facilitate hanging and navigation in flight.

About rabies: like almost all mammals, bats can get rabies. But less than half of a percent ever get the disease. Even bats with rabies, normally only bite in self defense. This is a real good reason to "look, but don't touch." Although scary, the fear of rabies is much greater than the actual risk. In perspective, in the past 50 years only 48 US residents have gotten rabies from bats. In comparison, 20 Americans die every year from dog attacks.

Besides, vampire bats are only in Central America. Three species of bats prick the skin and then lap up the blood. The anticoagulant they secrete has been synthesized and is used for human heart patients.

Even bat droppings are useful. Guano in caves supports a whole ecosystem of unique organisms. Guano is mined to provide a popular garden fertilizer.

There are many reasons bats are interesting. Besides, my friend, now that she has seen Bat Pup up close, thinks it is cute.

For more info http://www.batcon.org/

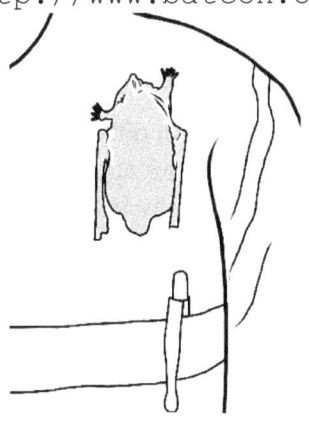

It's Not Just Puppies and Kittens

What Makes Me Cry...

A couple of weeks ago, I got the kind of call I love. And hate.

The call was from a wildlife biologist, with an invitation to go in an abandoned mine to survey for white nose syndrome in bats. Well, actually they wanted some of my anesthesia gas and perhaps my expertise in killing things humanely. I pushed for the invitation into the mine. See, I love bats.

White Nose Syndrome is killing millions of bats. It has just recently been found to be associated with a newly identified fungus, *Geomyces destructans.* It is named White Nose Syndrome (WNS) because the fungus appears and grows into white tufts on the muzzles of infected bats. Bats probably get it mostly from other bats; however, it is likely humans could transport spores from contaminated sites to new sites on clothing, footwear or gear.

This is why I haven't been in mines or caves lately. Nobody who truly understands WNS wants to spread it anywhere it is not. But I haven't been in any mines or caves since the disease broke out in 2006 and I do know a tad about the disinfection process. Normally, from Fish and Wildlife or the US Forest Service's point of view, I am the ideal volunteer. I like bats, so I am willing to go out in the woods, in mines or caves, at night and not only am I free, but I have had my rabies vaccines. (The risk of rabies from bats is much lower than once thought but still real.)

Anyway, the fungus only grows at cooler temperatures, so the bats are susceptible while hibernating. Many bats die during hibernation, but biologists don't really understand if the fungus causes the deaths or just interfere with hibernation which causes the bats to die. Either way it is bad.

Bats eat up to 4,500 insects a night. Every night. Every bat. So a million bats in a large colony must eat about the national debt worth of bugs in a season. Okay, so the math says they only eat about half a trillion bugs in a season. If those bugs are not eaten by bats, more bad news chemicals will have to be used. More chemicals mean more ecosystem disruption.

Since 2006, over a million cave-hibernating bats have died with WNS. But we are hopeful as we hike in and unlock the gate. Our mine inspector goes first to check for human safety. This is a known hibernaculum for endangered Indiana Bats.

White Nose Syndrome has never been reported in Ohio or Kentucky, but we all feel like it is coming. It has been confirmed in 15 states and Canada. This February and March, Ohio state and federal biologists have surveyed mines and results have been clear.

We enter to see over 1300 bats hibernating. Little brown bats, Indiana bats and some tri-colored bats were present. At first it looks okay, but then the biologist spots an Indiana bat with fluffy white around his nose. The biologist takes a tape impression of the fungus, but leaves the endangered bat. I spot two more non endangered bats which look like they have the disease. I do what I was brought to for and the bats are sent to the lab for histopathology.

We quietly leave the mine, but we all know what the lab will confirm a week later. WNS is in Ohio and millions more bats will die. It will affect all of us. And tonight, I shed a tear.

From the press release: People can help slow the spread of White-nose Syndrome and reduce disturbance to bats by staying out of caves and mines. Ohioans who observe more than six dead bats or large numbers of bats flying outside in the winter (less than 40°F), especially near a cave or mine where bats are known to hibernate, should report those observations to the ODNR Division of Wildlife at wildinfo@dnr.state.oh.us, or 1-800-WILDLIFE (945-3543). Utilize the same precautions when dealing with any wild animal, avoid touching wildlife and do not pick up sick or dead bats.

For more information about WNS and Ohio bats, please visit www.fws.gov/whitenosesyndrome and www.wildohio.com.

Changing Colors

Fall is in the air. The crisp mornings mean the fall colors are beginning to think about coming out. While the changing color of the leaves has to do with uncovered pigments and saving chemicals for next year, there are animals that have color changes and differences also.

As fall progresses, normal white tail deer will get darker or grayer. Fawns lose their spots. All of the coats will be a thicker, denser coat that is better able to keep them warm. But some deer and other animals have color differences that have nothing to do with the weather.

Most deer are brown with some white, but variations in the amount of melanin produce different colors. Melanin is the chemical that produces skin color. Most animals have some, others none. These genetic changes mean deer can be anything from black to white with combinations in between. For deer there are five colors: normal, piebald, white, albino and melanistic.

A brown deer with significant white on it is called a piebald, like the horse of the same color. This partially white deer is the most common color mutation. Some of the cells produce normal dark pigment so some areas are normal and some are white. In a piebald it seems to be more that white pigment is produced than no pigment. So, a piebald is amelanistic, not albinos. These have been estimated to occur about one in two to three thousand deer. Often this genetic combination comes with dwarfism and other genetic problems.

Around Seneca Army Depot in New York, there is a concentration of white whitetails. Sometimes these are called ghost deer. This is a fenced population that is strictly controlled. From one white deer in 1951, there are now more than 200 white ones. These are white, but not albinos. Their color occurs the same way a piebald does only all over their body. The fawns can have tan or cream fur with the same markings as normal fawns, but by two years old the coats fade to white.

In an albino, none of the cells produce melanin or color. They look white because they lack any pigment. Albino deer will be all white with pink eyes. Sometimes the ears look pink because the blood vessels can be seen through the skin. White rats are albinos and the lack of pigment and red eyes make me think the eyes are empty. It can make them sensitive to light because they lack pigment to block light into their eyes. True albinos occur at about one to every 30,000 deer in the normal population.

The most rare are black or nearly black which is call melanistic. These skin cells produce too much of the melanin. This dark pigmentation will usually eliminate normal white marking. There is a growing herd in Texas and it is assumed there is some advantage to this gene make up. Melanistic deer are quite rare and may occur at on in 60-100,000 normal deer.

GAMC does a lot of wildlife rehabilitation and in my two and a half decades, I have seen one piebald deer and a single totally amelanistic hawk and one partial amelanistic. Oh, and quite a few pet albino rats.

SECTION 7: VET LIFE

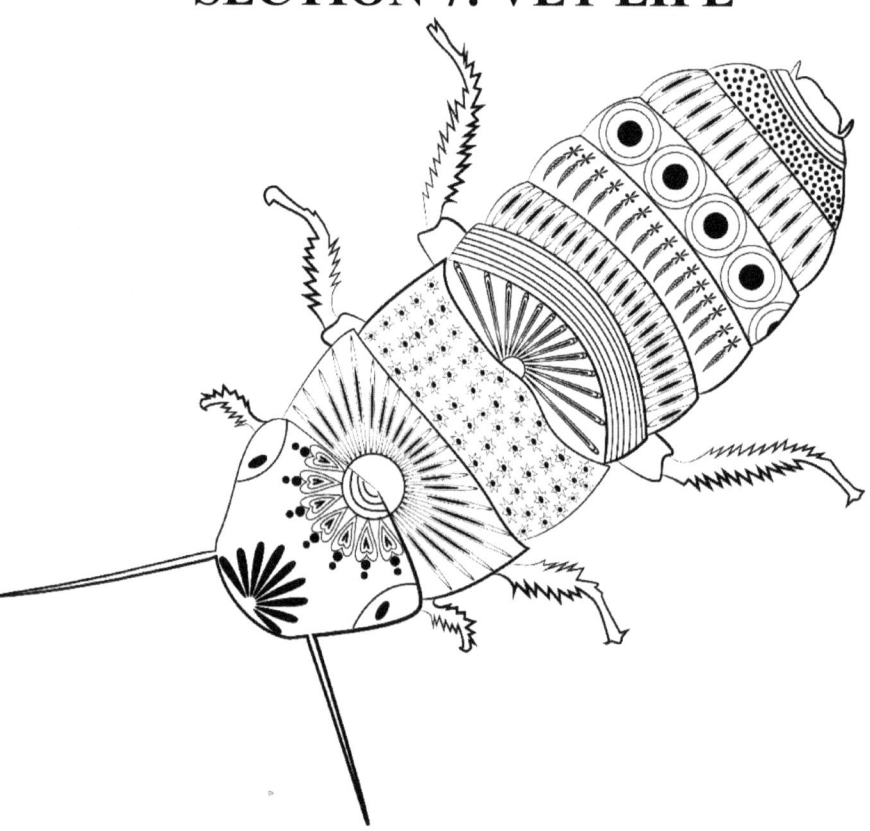

It's Not Just Puppies and Kittens

I woke up to a bad dream this morning, a...

    I woke up to a bad dream this morning, a nightmare actually. Someone I trusted had turned on me and then bragged about taking someone important and dear to me. As soon as possible, I made sure my folks were not leaving and then started thinking about loyalty.
    Many of us have pets, especially dogs, because of their loyalty. And a lot of quite famous people have commented on this quality of dogs. Sigmund Freud said "Dogs love their friends and bite their enemies, quite unlike people, who are incapable of pure love and always have to mix love and hate in their objective relations." Alexander Pope noted "Histories are more full of examples of the fidelity of dogs than of friends." John Billings writes "A dog is the only thing on earth that loves you more than he loves himself." I do see this loyalty in Ranger. He would protect his "big sister" if she needed it. (But to be totally honest, most times he could probably be "bought" with a treat and he totally thinks I can protect myself!)
    Loyalty may not be Ranger's big thing, but dog loyalty has been recognized for a long time. From Greek mythology, the great hunter Orion had a dog named Sirius. There is a constellation named Sirius with the star Sirius as the diamond in the collar. Orion's Sirius is a faithful companion. It is said if you dream of a dog, it may be you are longing for a loyal companion. The dog as a companion is a symbol of loyalty and trust. Indeed if the dog is accompanied by someone you know in your dream, that person may be the one receiving your feelings of loyalty and trust.
    But maybe loyalty is mostly a dog trait; according to recent events, it certainly does not seem to be a sports trait. There is a group on facebook called "If you want loyalty, get a dog." I don't think I will join. Even if I cannot be as loyal as a dog, I can still try. (And I do expect loyalty of my inner family and friends.) Indeed Gilda Radner puts it a little more bluntly "I think dogs are the most amazing creatures; they give unconditional love. For me they are the role model for being alive."
    "He is your friend, your partner, your defender, your dog. You are his life, his love, his leader. He will be yours, faithful and true, to the last

beat of his heart. You owe it to him to be worthy of such devotion."
Unknown

    Whether we are worthy of this devotion or not, there have been some remarkable stories of dog loyalty over the years. Greyfriar's Bobby kept a virtually constant watch over his owner's grave. Day and night, he stayed by the grave, leaving only to eat once a day. Bobby outlasted his master by fourteen years. Because it was consecrated ground, he could not be buried with his master. Bobby is buried just outside the gate with a headstone that reads, "Greyfriar's Bobby - died 14th January 1872 - aged 16 years - Let his loyalty and devotion be a lesson to us all."

    After he was lost on a family vacation in 1923, Bobbie, a collie/Shepard mix, found his way home from Indiana to Oregon. The 2,800 mile trip took him six months. Bobbie's faithfulness was noted in newspaper articles and in Ripley's Believe it or Not.

    There have been some modern day tales of extreme loyalty. In Japan, a dog would go with his master to the train station every morning and return to the train station each afternoon to greet him after work. After the man died, the dog returned to the same spot at the train station every day for the next nine years. The dog became a lesson to the local people about love, compassion and unyielding loyalty. Now a bronze statue of the dog sits in his waiting spot outside the station as a permanent reminder of his devotion and love.

    This brings new meaning to "Friends Fur-ever."

    Perhaps that is why, upon waking from this unpleasant dream this morning, I reached for Ranger to make sure he was there.

    And, of course, he was.

    For the villain of my dream, a final quote from Mark Twain: "If you pick up a starving dog and make him prosperous, he will not bite you; that is the principal difference between a dog and a man."

It's Not Just Puppies and Kittens

It's Not Just Puppies and Kittens

What a day!

And I don't mean that in a good way. Nothing major, but yesterday was just one of those days!

It started the night before with a couple of capsules of Nyquil. Then I slept through the phone call that canceled school. When my husband woke me up, I acknowledged him and went back to sleep. When M'Kinzy came in an hour later, I was sound asleep.

Then a phone call. I find the anticipation of bad news is never as bad as the specific bad news. (Note to self: teach this to the new doctor.) Mindy had three of her four puppies but they were dead. She had been sitting on them.

I ordered x-rays as I got up to head in. Unfortunately communication was not achieved and the x-rays I asked for were not done by the time I got in. Finally, radiographs are up and the puppy seems to have a broken neck in the uterus.

Obviously, surgery was off to a late start, but the few surgeries went well. Then we added on a surgery for a shelter dog that had removed its sutures too early.

Okay, so surgery prep didn't go quite so well, because I had decided to fix the bottom of the surgery prep cabinet. But it had a bit of rust and the base had to be replaced, which meant parts to be bought. That meant it was still lying on the floor. All of the contents were in boxes on top of the new cabinet boxes we haven't had time to put up yet.

During this time Mindy got some more drugs and time, but still no puppy. I donned sterile gloves and could feel two back feet, but could not manipulate the puppy out. Mindy rested and I tried several more times throughout the day.

Meanwhile, appointments started. Nothing major: puppy plans, a couple of annuals, some allergies and ears. Then a parvovirus puppy came in. Actually, two parvo puppies, because when we questioned the owners the other pup was not eating also. This would make three parvo cases in our parvo ward, because one of Tuesday's surgeries had not been properly vaccinated and broke with the disease on Wednesday. (The incubation period is three to ten days, so it was sick before we saw it, but still.)

The renal failure dog is doing great, but it is time to change his catheter. And Mindy is a go for surgery and she needs an IV catheter. At this point, I sent the staff for a forbidden substance: a bag of Ruffles. (Please, don't tell my MD, I only do it about once a year. And I did order a salad for lunch, didn't eat it until after 8:00 pm and it was a regular not the antipasto I wanted. Okay, so I took it to share and friends added stuff to make it edible.)

Then one of the AARF (Ashland Animal Rescue Foundation) dogs rescued from the shelter started showing signs of respiratory disease. (I am so glad they have their own ward away from the other dogs.) But we can't put her in the respiratory isolation ward because there are two puppies with pneumonia in there. So we decide to step up the move-cages-into-physical-therapy-room project to top priority. That of course, means the aquarium project has to be moved up on the list because aquarium stuff is sitting on the cage rack.

About 5:00 p.m., I realized I needed to call the Social Security administration. W-2's were imminently due and they had locked me out of the system just because I put in my password wrong 3 times. And yesterday they closed for some minor snow event of a few feet of snow. And today nobody would answer. But I had to get in to finish W-2's or start all over.

Did I mention the kennel drain for the shelter/AARF dogs was slow to almost backed up? After surgery, Dennis resumed work on this project, but while the auger ran well, water did not. And my contractor is out of town on a week long project.

Meanwhile, with the carpet people, contractors, cleaners and workers at the house, we had not had time to go for supplies lately. So GAMC, which runs on Mountain Dew, was out of this precious substance.

Seems a few things didn't get put on the list until yesterday, because, well, we ran out of toilet paper.

It was just one of those days.

It's Not Just Puppies and Kittens

I went to school for a long time to be able to do this.

Paprika is headed to another vet today. He actually has been to see quite a few veterinarians lately. He came to us from North Carolina, where he actually had been sent home to die.

Pap is only four or five years old, but his kidneys are failing. He was first sick back in November and got IV fluids, but he didn't get enough to get his blood toxins back to normal. Pap was in and out of the hospital in North Carolina three different times for fluids without ever getting enough fluids over a long enough period to lower his toxin levels to normal. That is the first thing we did when we got him in. He was on IV fluids for a little over a week. Follow up blood work showed that with the fluid flushing out his system, he was almost normal.

(I suspect Pap was given antifreeze which killed off a lot of cells in his kidneys. Because he had so few functioning kidney cells, he cannot get rid of the normal byproducts of life. These toxins build up and get increasingly more, well, toxic. After a point his brain and heart cannot handle the level of toxins and he would die.)

IV fluids were a huge first step, but not the only step for Pap. Pap is a Champion Field trial beagle and is used for stud service. His puppies have been field champions also. The owners would really like to have Pap, but if he cannot be around, they would like some more puppies.

Since Pap had been sick since November, we didn't know if he would produce any normal sperm. And also, the sperm had to be viable enough to collect and store. On a recent day, we collected a sample and found normal, living sperm. It did seem like the numbers were a little low, but honestly this is better than we had hoped for at this time.

Pap then made the trip to Louisville to get sperm collected for freezing and long term storage. His sperm was healthy and showed forward mobility, but he could not produce enough sperm to collect and store. When sperm is frozen and stored about half of the sperm die. When you start with billions, half lost is not a big deal. Starting with a low number means even less after storage. The reproductive specialist did not think there would be enough to have a reasonable chance at puppies.

Collecting, freezing, storing and implanting sperm is not a cheap process either, so it was doubly foolish if it was not going to work.

So, Pap came back to GAMC to continue his fluid therapy to give his system enough time to start to produce sperm again. (Sperm are not essential to life and the body had quit making them, because it was trying so hard just to stay alive.)

But Pap was looking great. He was eating better than he had been in months and "Jeff" was in heat and they really wanted Jeff/Pap puppies. So assisted breeding was attempted. Pap wanted to, but he just didn't have the energy for the 45 minute process.

Artificial Insemination was the next step. Pap rested overnight, but was still quite interested in being a pupdad. Although most vets can do fresh collection and AI, with today's schedule we decided Pap would be better off going to another hospital to get a sample. He will be coming back for more fluids and continued care.

In Pap's case, it really will take a team of trained veterinarians to produce puppies.

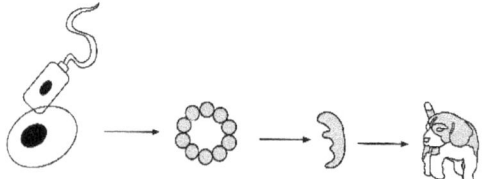

The One that Got Away!

I hate interviewing prospective employees! Over the years, I have hired some real non-winners. And missed some great employees. The not-good employees have stolen from me, lied to me, forged checks and various other stressful things. People we have passed over have become great employees at other clinics, veterinarians, lawyers, medical doctors, educators and many others. Sometimes I see prior employees at Wal-mart or McDonalds. Sometimes I hear stories about how I didn't hire someone who is now a professional. Veterinary clinics do not tend to pay well, so we are competing with fast food and retail and tend to pull from a lot of students.

The job is fun and not at all boring, so for every position, we get maybe a hundred applicants. Sifting through that many applications is problematic at best. The first pass through the written applications is the easy part. Improperly completed forms and ones that only say "see resume" get a major black mark. A huge black mark is gained by refusing to deal with dog poop or something equally prevalent at a veterinary practice. (It is always good to know a little something about the place you are applying to.)

After the written applications are pared down, we invite the remaining applicants for a group interview. Here we try to gauge how the prospective employee deals with typical situations, thinks on their feet and deals with stress. We try to be honest and open about the job. There are lots of great things about working in a veterinary place and lots of not so great things. It is amazing how many people think working here is all about playing with puppies and kittens all day every day! If you think it is rough to do a group interview as an applicant, it is; it is equally not easy to pick someone to spend many of your waking hours in a short amount of interview time.

From the group interview, a select few do a 'working interview'. This is where the person comes in and works for a 4-hour shift. (Things can get hectic and sometimes this time extends.) Working interviews are usually where I get to meet people for the first time. I found out long ago people will act more naturally around their future peers than they will The Doctor.

Working interviews can be a lot of fun for both the person and the team. We had one kennel cleaning applicant who never set down his coffee cup the whole time. Fun to watch on close circuit TV, but not hired. Another crawled in the cage with the animal instead of feeding, walking and cleaning. There are some who didn't realize just how much physical work it actually takes to work with animals. Some are even afraid of animals. But most are just young. (Hint: six months or more at McDonalds looks good on an entry level application.)

I recently re-met one of our non-hires. He is a quite capable professional, but he tells a story about working for me for a day. I guess a day could be correct when you figure a half day could be 6-8 hours around here. He says we gave him leather gloves that came up to his shoulders and told him to move this huge eagle and then clean the cage that took hours. He is much younger than I and I am certain his memory is better than mine, but I really only remember two bald eagles coming to Guardian Animal. Since eagles were federally protected, endangered and violations punishable by jail time for me, I am quite certain a new employee would have never gotten near an eagle.

Again with that memory thing, but the gloves we have now come right to your elbow. Being able to move your elbow and move quickly is essential, because even though it might not have been an eagle and memory and time enlarges things and tales, a red-tailed hawk or a barred owl are both quite formidable opponents. I have had both go through the leather gloves and into my arm. We must have been impressed to allow a new recruit to touch one.

I don't know why, but in the end, we didn't hire this person. We spent a bit of time talking with him and on his own, he went straight from Guardian Animal back to his prior job at the movie theater. But we gave him a story that has lasted for 15 years. And sometimes, that is the best thing we do for prospective employees: we remind them to stay in school, go to college and/or get a different job.

But I think, Mr. Superintendent, it is about time for a new adventure for a new story. Keep some time on your schedule open. We will be in touch.

Please, don't pray for patience for me!

I don't have a lot of patience. Basically, I am okay with that. I do not expect any more from others than I expect from myself, but I was hoping to find enough patience to work with a new intern. She is pleasant and bright and I thought I could work with someone who was younger and needed coaching. I truly enjoy teaching and like the enthusiasm of young people learning.

Well, I have spoken of this intern many times with my best friend. Unfortunately, I also spoke of her with folks who are just friends. Therefore, last Monday night, I resolved to only be positive and not say anything negative, especially in front of the staff.

Well, that lasted about an hour on Tuesday morning! I know she needs confidence, so I have been allowing her to do pre-surgery physical exams. She can take all the time she needs and has no pressure of their owner (or me). If there is anything really wrong, I already know about it or surgery would not have been scheduled.

Copper was my third surgery of the morning. Things were going well, partly due to the fact that I enjoy surgery. I pleasantly (no really, I actually was trying hard) coached my intern on the fact that taking seven minutes to do a physical exam was fine (I do a very through exam in a minute or two), but she might want to do it while I was in surgery and not while I was waiting for my next surgery.

During my second surgery, she examined Copper for his castration and said he had some white froth in his mouth. Blood work was quite normal and I explained this was probably due to the atropine premed which dries secretions and therefore makes saliva thick. (I am still calm, even though I KNOW this was covered in vet school.)

Everything was going well. I was even a little proud of myself that we were almost finished with surgery for the day and I was remaining supportive and positive. That thought quickly vanished as I glanced at my surgery. Since I had already scrubbed in and donned sterile attire, I first questioned my surgical assistant.

"Dennis, is there only one testicle?"

It's Not Just Puppies and Kittens

Dennis knew and highly supported my resolve to be more positive and said "oh, surely not. I am sure there are two."

But there were not. Well, there were, because there always is, but they can be anywhere from the external inguinal ring to the internal ring to right beside the kidney or anywhere in between. In short, NOT an easy surgery and one that requires a MUCH different preparation. Surgical prep that had NOT been done and now Cooper was in surgery on anesthesia.

I called her in. Not very positively, I asked her if she had checked for both testicles. She said she thought there were two.

Somewhat loudly, I questioned, "What you can't count to two?" We proceeded to determine she had not bothered to check. "So, we are doing a castration and you don't bother to check the site of the surgery?"

I would like to say this was said in the most positive manner, but I cannot. The staff became one with the woodwork and trim. After I completed the surgery and Copper was fine, I told Dennis I felt I had failed because I did not remain calm and positive. He said he had stuck up for her a lot of times, but this time she deserved to be chewed out.

Three days later when I calmed down enough to talk about it again, she asked if I "didn't find it yucky back there?"

I told her, "no, I didn't, because it is part of the job that must be done."

I know we get patience by practicing patience, but I have been happy with the trade-off of strong professionalism and perfectionist tendencies toward my patient care. More pets live and do better because of my impatience with substandard care. I am even a little proud, even if there are times I would like to be a little more nurturing. But please, please stop praying for patience for me, I have really had about all I can stand.

It's Not Just Puppies and Kittens

Do I Need to Worry?

"My daughter was bitten by her friend's dog last night, do I need to worry about rabies?"

The caller was a friend with a daughter the same age as mine. Both girls are happy, pleasant preteens, so I fully understand the fear that the question of rabies brings up. In different situations, different answers will apply.

First a disclaimer: your human health care provider is the one who needs to give advice for humans. All I can do is provide some information about rabies, because I hope I see more than my MD. Rabies is not a very fun disease in anything, but to think of it in a child makes me sick.

Unless blood is spurting everywhere, wash the wound first. This should be thorough and include soap and water, in other words not just running under water. The single most important thing to prevent rabies transmission is to clean the wound. Don't think small wounds are less likely to be a problem. Wounds that do not break the skin and bleed can be more likely to transmit rabies. Since there is no blood, people are less likely to clean them, but the virus can still migrate to the nerves and from there begin the slow migration to the brain. Indeed that wait can be six months to multiple years.

After first aid, a trip to your health care provider, or at least a call to the county health department, is in order. Any deep or puncture wound needs appropriate antibiotics. Whatever is left in the medicine cabinet from your last sickness is NOT okay. Cats especially, but also dogs, have bacteria in their mouths that is not treated by normal antibiotics. And while rabies is rare, tetanus is extremely common. Make certain your tetanus is up to date.

If you visit your doctor's office, their staff will notify the health department. Otherwise, you will need to. The health department will visit the pet and impose a 10 to 15 day quarantine. This can be at the shelter, a vet or sometimes in the home. While this short amount of time is not enough to know if the pet has rabies (remember the multiple years to develop); it is enough to know if the pet has rabies in the salivary glands, at the time of the bite, and therefore transmitting rabies, because the pet will be sick within this time frame.

Why don't we just treat all bites as though the animal had rabies?

Great question! Although the disease is significant, the treatment is not inconsequential either. Huge amounts of antiserum are injected around the already painful bite wound. I don't know about his daughter, but injecting 2 to 5 ounces into my daughter's face would not be on her top ten list!

Then the reactions are significant. Allergic reactions, serum sickness and sometimes even death happen with antiserum treatments. Don't get me wrong, if there was a good chance of rabies in the bite wound, I would be sitting on my daughter while she was injected.

What tells professionals which bites should be treated?

A whole host of things are taken into account. How many rabies cases have been in the area? What is the closest recent case of rabies? How long has it been since rabies has been diagnosed in the county? What type of animal was it? Was it a provoked or unprovoked bite? Has it been vaccinated? Was it by a veterinarian? Are the vaccinations current?

In some cases the health department can force an unvaccinated animal to be euthanized and the head submitted for rabies testing. This is necessary because of the human life that is at risk. The longer between a rabid bite and treatment, the less likely it is treatment will work.

So, if it seems this parent is between a rock and a hard place, they are. Nobody wants to have another person's family pet put to sleep, but neither do they want to watch their child die of rabies.

Once again, the take home message is vaccinate your pet.

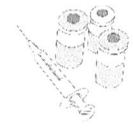

I Miss my Technology.

Our internet is down. And in trying to reset our internet, the phones (which are voice over internet protocol) went down. I feel so disconnected. And helpless. And unproductive. It seems everything revolves around technology.

Technology has become such a part of practice that I cannot imagine veterinary medicine without it. Client records, prescriptions, bills, reminders and more are all on the computer. A different computer and program cover accounts payable or bills, online accounts and more.

It seems technology is everywhere: laboratory equipment, heart monitors, automatic blood pressure monitors, ECG machines, ultrasounds and diagnostic equipment. Right now my staff is taking radiographs. A 400milliamp machine emits x-ray beams and lights up phosphorescence crystals to allow for a picture of internal objects. Speaking of pictures, digital cameras allow for photos to be in computer records, charts, facebook updates and documentation of progress. Another benefit to smart phones is the use of the built in camera. At our last vet meeting in West Liberty, all the vets had their cell phones out showing off cases. (GAMC won the bragging contest, because we had post op photos of a PDA heart surgery that was not only alive, but up and standing.)

I miss the basic internet and phones.

The internet is up on my computer at all times. I have a facebook account where I post animal-related articles and miscellaneous items. Several 'magazines' crowd my email instead of my inbox. Many of my articles are researched with internet help. Online software allows me to make Prezis for presentations.

Email is used for lab reports, non urgent comms and daily veterinary news. (I also find it is a great way to communicate with school folks.) I usually log on to email first thing in the morning and keep it up in the background all day.

Our phones are down. That means we have no incoming or out going communications, but even so, technology is in heavy use around the hospital. As I type this on my computer, technology allows the computers to talk to each other so the reception staff knows what has been done in the back. Hopefully before the article deadline, technology will allow for this computer to email this article to the editor.

I try to do at least one Continuing Education class a month via the internet. Even our ECG's go out over a special modem via phone lines to a cardiologist.

We even have "smart" thermostats that allow the kennels and wards to remain at a constant temp while the waiting room can be less heated on the weekends and nights.

My planner is now on the computer. Not only is it lighter to carry around when (if) it syncs to my smart phone, but it will not allow me to drop a task that didn't get done today. And it knows every Friday and Monday, I have an article deadline. It also knows when taxes are due and reminds me in enough time to get them out.

As a matter of fact, the W-2's went to the Social Security Administration by the magic of internet. State unemployment reports are now completed online and federal tax deposits are made online.

New in the works for us (as soon as the new internet connections are all talking) is an internet Pet Portal. Clients will be able to go online and check the status of vaccines and reminders. Reminders can be sent by email. (If we don't have your email address, call or email us.)

I sleep better at night because I know the security system will alert me to ANY problems. (But does the fancy security and alarm system really have to incessantly tell us the phones were down? That alarm is loud, annoying, cannot be turned off and gosh, we already know the phones aren't working.)

Technology is a wonderful thing. After three hours, we have phones back and internet some places, but not in my office. I just wish it was working. Now.

I am truly glad the security system has got its connection to the security company again. And that my stethoscope only needs me to make it work.

It's Not Just Puppies and Kittens

(Turns out my computer and the router were fighting over the same IP address. Things would just be a lot better in the world if all could share peacefully.)

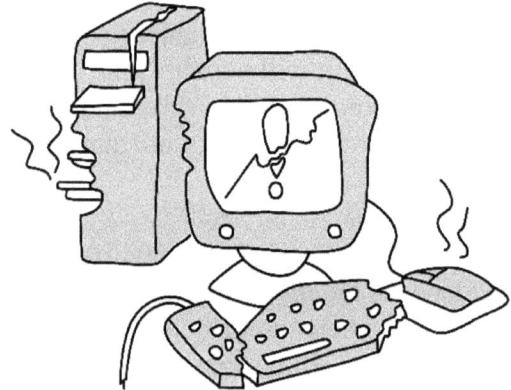

It's Not Just Puppies and Kittens

Beck is Going to Germany.

Maybe. Well, he is, but maybe not with his owner. Beck is a basenji and his dad is a medic in the Army. Beck's dad has been transferred to a unit in Germany. Since Beck was checked out in Hawaii before he left, everything should be good to fly out, right? Not so easy anymore.

Rules have changed on both sides of the ocean. The consolidation of the European Union is supposed to make international travel easier. If you are already in Europe, this is probably true. The new rules make it difficult to say the least.

Several weeks ago, Beck's grandmom called to see if we could do health certificates for a dog to fly. I am an accredited veterinarian in the state of Kentucky, so the staff said I could. Unfortunately, it did not register to anyone to mention to senior staff that this was an international flight. An international flight requires an international health certificate and every country's import requirements are different. Beck arrived at my office in the late afternoon on a Thursday before travel on an early Tuesday morning flight.

An international health certificate often starts with a call to the State Department for that country to ask what the current requirements for animal importation are. (They don't work after 4:30pm.) Next problem encountered was that last summer, all of the rules for USDA veterinarians changed. Under the old rules you took a class, passed a test and were accredited for life. Well, someone figured out not all of us remembered everything from that class twenty or more years ago. So the system was thrown out, but they did not expect the number of veterinarians to apply under the new system and registration is taking about a year longer than expected.

So first thing Friday morning, we called the office to check on my accreditation status. Great news! They have my registration done and soon I have an enrollment form with my new number on it. I am to put this on the International Health Certificate form 7001 (or is it form 7006?). Anyway, our forms don't have that number. We were supposed to order forms preprinted with accountability numbers. Nobody told us and not enough time for that, so we download a form and complete it no less than three times before Frankfort says it is okay. (We faxed it to them to proof twice.)

Back to the requirements to enter Germany, Beck had to be free of contagious disease and have had a microchip prior to receiving a rabies vaccine and the vaccine must be done 30 days before travel. Rabies was given in December in Hawaii by the Army post vet. Good.

Beck has a microchip, but the microchip is not the European standard microchip. We contact the manufacturer of the microchip to check to see if Beck's chip can be read in Germany. The chip is not ISO compatible. Beck cannot now get another microchip because of the 30 day requirement for the rabies. But the manufacturer has a solution: they will rent Beck's dad a chip scanner and return his hefty deposit when the scanner is returned. (Thank you, FEDEX, but wow, what a fee.)

Whew! Problem solved. Uh, wait. The person at the USDA/APHIS office didn't tell us the international original (blue ink only) health certificate had to be signed in Frankfort. The fax was not acceptable. (Don't forget the certificate has to be within 10 days of travel to be valid.) I am certain Beck's dad wanted to make one last trip to Frankfort, KY before going to Frankfurt, Germany. But it is better to make the trip than to start over.

So, with hours to spare, Beck is cleared to travel on an international flight. And a pet traveling with their owner is much safer than alone as cargo. We tried to call to see how Beck was doing with German, but remembered he was a basenji. They don't bark.

When we finally did get a hold of the grandmom, Beck was denied boarding because the airline was not prepared to do an international transfer. Beck stayed. Since Beck's dad had called the airline before arriving, he was a tad annoyed.

It's Not Just Puppies and Kittens

It's Not Just Puppies and Kittens

Have You Ever Treated . . . ?

I am coaching Russell McDowell Elementary Science Olympiad so, of course, the kids asked. To be fair, I often get asked what is the weirdest thing I have ever treated.

I am never prepared for this question. I just treat whatever comes in the door. I don't think any of the creatures are strange. Some are just different.

But some are definitely different! Not everyone chooses a playful puppy or a cute kitten.

You can cuddle with a hamster, guinea pig or other pocket pets. Some can even be trained. One girl is extremely impressed I spayed a hamster.

Birds are common exotic pets. Larger birds such as parrots or cockatoos have intelligence and emotions. (The intelligence of a seven-year-old and the emotions of a two-year-old.) They can learn to mimic and speak. Their long lives are both an advantage and disadvantage. Even parakeets or budgies can live to be 15 to 30 years on a proper non-seed diet. The advanced intelligence means they can be very bonded to their human owners. Sometimes too much so. And some of them are older than I am!

Reptiles and amphibians are definitely not cuddly, but are high on the cool factor. There is something fascinating about watching a lizard hunt crickets or a snake eat a mouse. And how cool is a pet that carries its house on their back?

The husbandry or caging and feeding requires research and experience. It would almost seem like getting a happy herptile is an ongoing test of one's ability to provide a great habitat.

We also do wildlife rehabilitation and see a number of animals come and go. I almost never get attached to these because they are wild animals and will be released. However, I had a baby brown bat that I bottle fed for several weeks. When it died of a vitamin C deficiency before we understood that it was important, I cried for hours. Still the bobcat, otter, fox and coyote were special.

But the kids are studying Arthropods and insects, so of course they asked. We did have pet millipedes for a while. They were actually good pets. High on the cool factor, but easy to take care of. They didn't bite, could be handled and ate vegetable leftovers from the kitchen, which gave me a good excuse not to eat all my salad.

I will not say my favorite animal in the world is a cockroach, but when one came into the clinic with a torn leg, I not only fixed it, but felt sorry for it.

My daughter had a fascination with spiders when she was younger. The cob spider under the bathroom sink had a name and was forbidden to be killed. This led to numerous (so far unheeded) requests for a tarantula. Tarantulas are probably the most common pet spiders and we have treated them as pets.

We had a black widow spider at Guardian Animal for more than three years. I didn't set out to have a black widow, but when she came she was already in a sealed unbreakable plastic container. It just seemed wrong to kill her when she couldn't hurt us. So, she stayed and we rigged up a way to safely feed her. Somewhere along the way, we got attached to Cruela. We would gather around watch as she spun a web around her food before eating it. The staff would catch grasshoppers while walking dogs or buy her crickets from the pet store. And when she died, we missed her. Sometimes years later, we still do.

As for other weird stuff over the years, well, Fish and Wildlife dropped off a Caiman crocodile, deer, hawks, owls and a river otter. There have been goats, pot bellied pigs, ferrets, rabbits, prairie dogs, hedgehogs, mountain lions, African lion cubs, black bears, Rheas (South American ostriches) African ostriches, Emus, hummingbirds, and even fish.

All things bright and beautiful.
All creatures great and small.

All things wise and wonderful.
The Lord God made them all.

Answers to the Fourth Graders

Last year, before we had been in the building a week, we had my daughter's fourth grade class visit. It was chaos. Clients' appointments ran over, staff was busy and emergencies showed up. Of course, the patients were given priority and I barely had time to say hello to the teacher. The kids were happy to see the waiting room, but I had hoped we could do more to teach them.

This year we had two classes visit and things went much better. Still there were some questions that did not get an adequate answer at the time (something about almost sixty kids at GAMC at a time.) I thought I would give the answers here. By the way, I will leave it to you to figure out the questions, but after a tour, the kids were split up into groups that went to different stations.

There are five densities seen on radiographs. From most dense or white to least dense or black, they are metal, bone, fluid, fat and air. Puppies cannot be adequately seen on radiographs or x-rays until the bones have enough calcium to show up. Otherwise they are the same density as fluid, organs or tissue and you cannot determine they are definitely present until 45 days of pregnancy. Since the dog was only 41 days, she still might be pregnant, but the uterus was difficult to find.

Heartworms are carried by mosquitos to dogs and cats. They live and grow under the skin and then, if not killed by a preventive, move to the heart and lungs. No, that is not good for your pet's heart to have several foot long worms in it. Yes, we can kill the foot long worms, but it is better to keep them from getting them in the first place.

Examinations are important, because the animals cannot tell me what is going on or where it hurts. Veterinarians listen, move, look, smell and touch, but most of all we think and use our knowledge to put things together. Yes, I occasionally do get to taste when they give me a kiss.

You cannot touch your nose after you scrub, because that defeats the whole purpose of sterile surgery. This was not understood until the late 1800's, but tiny, invisible microbes can do some really bad things. Making a surgical wound and contaminating it with bacteria, will cause infections. It really doesn't matter how much your nose itches after you scrub in. And, yes, all of your hair is supposed to fit under the cap, so a stray hair doesn't fall into the surgical field.

When they shake, you will get wet. After all that is why they call it a bath; it is wet. Just because we use a hydrosurge, which is like a Jacuzzi jet, doesn't mean there is no water.

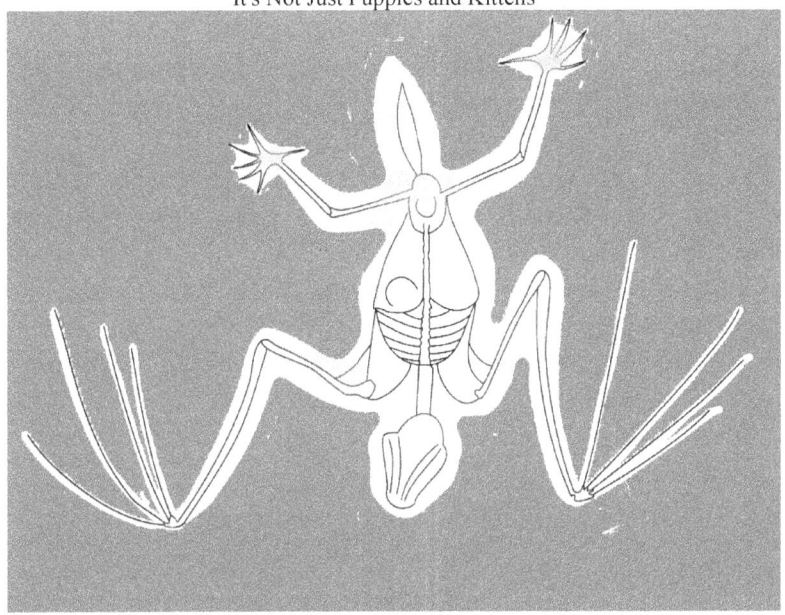

You have to go to four years of graduate school after you go to regular college. Admission is extremely competitive. It is harder to get into veterinary school than medical school; there are many more medical schools than veterinary colleges. Good grades, high test scores and lots of science and math are required for all doctors. Human doctors and veterinary doctors both tend to work more than they should. MD's generally get paid more than DVM's.

No, I do not. The variety of species and problems I work on and (mostly) solve and the families I help mean every day is new and interesting and fun. From the Life is Good® company:

Do what you like.
Like what you do®
And I do.

It's Not Just Puppies and Kittens

To Sleep– Forever is dedicated to Crockett and the many others. This article was in the Daily Independent and written in 1997.

I just ended a friend's suffering. And his life. It is a sad time and I shed more than a few tears as did his family, but it is also one of the wonderful things we have available in veterinary medicine that we do not have in human medicine.

See, this dog had a disease condition I could not fix. His parents had taken him to specialists and we had done all we could to increase his quality and quantity of life.

Unfortunately, there are limits and eventually nothing more can be done, but end the suffering.

> **Euthanasia is a personal desision. No one else can make the decision for you.**

The pet's suffering usually does not even begin to match the owner's pain of making the decision to end a pet's life. Some conditions that look very bad to an owner may be quite treatable. Others cannot be treated or the expense of 'human quality' medicine is more than owners are willing to do. Some treatments are very expensive, especially when compared to the expected outcome.

Regardless the decision is never easy for any pet parent. Owners often feel guilty whether they make the decision to euthanize or feel they prolonged the suffering too long. Hindsight often makes it look obvious we should have taken the other road. Guilt is a normal phase of grieving even when it is unjustified.

Often animals will look better on their way into the veterinarian for euthanasia. I believe this is a factor of the owner's feelings that the pets pick up and knowledge that the pain or weakness is almost over. I don't know how they know, but it happens often enough there must be something in the human animal bond from the animal's point of view.

At the veterinarian's office, expect to sign some paperwork. Our form says that you do want the animal permanently put to sleep and that the animal hasn't bitten anyone in the last ten days and to the best of your knowledge, your animal does not have rabies. This paperwork helps with the communication process. (Remember James Herriot 'putting the dog to sleep' and then finding out later the owners wanted it to sleep and not die.) This also alerts veterinarians if the body must be specially handled to protect you or our staff members.

When we euthanize a pet, we give them an injection of a concentrated barbiturate solution. Pets with a normal cardiovascular system go to sleep in less than 20 seconds. Pets with poor circulation may take longer, but at no time feel any pain. After they are asleep, their heart stops and their lungs stop and they die.

The only thing they feel is perhaps a brief excitement or pleasure. This is what the drug addicts are trying to reach when they abuse these drugs. Sometimes the pets will do strange things (just like those addicts) right before they go to sleep. Although the pets feel nothing but pleasure, the people can interpret these actions as pain. Nothing could be farther from the truth, but that visual picture can be disturbing.

Sometimes after the animal is dead, muscles can contract and cause the body to move. This is the same as the gruesome frog leg and electrode experiment that we used to do in high school. The animal is truly brain dead, but the muscles still may contract.

Animals also sense the owner's anxiety and become tense themselves. The problems I have had with euthanasia have always been when the parents are around. These are the reasons that any decision to be with a pet during the process should be carefully thought out. (I personally recommend against it. But as the last thing they hear, I always tell the pet that their family loved them.)

The five steps of greiving are
1. **Denial**
2. **Bargaining**
3. **Anger or Guilt**
4. **Sorrow or Grief**
5. **Resolution**

But from the animal's point of view, everything was quick and easy. A slight injection, pleasure and then a final permanent end to suffering. Euthanasia is not something I like to do. I doubt if any veterinarian likes to do it. But it is sometimes the best of all available alternatives. And there are certainly worse ways to die. Because sometimes, all the medicine in the world cannot fix everything. But that doesn't mean I don't cry. I really like the quote from James Herriot. "Like all vets I hated doing this, painless though it was, but to me there has always been a comfort in the knowledge that the last thing these helpless animals knew was the sound of a friendly voice and the touch of a gentle hand."

The word worship could come
from the word to be dog-like.
They live only for us.
They forgive us for anything and everything.
They adore us in every way.

How could we help but love
something that worships us?
And how could we not miss every single one that is gone.

MJ Wixsom, DVM MS

SECTION 8: OUT AND ABOUT

It's Not Just Puppies and Kittens

The 2011 Race to the Sky Sled dog race is over .

The dogs, mushers, officials, veterinarians and volunteers are headed back to their normal lives. For a week people of all types came together to celebrate cold weather and working dogs.

This year's veterinary crew came from Washington, Ohio, Montana and Kentucky. All dogs were given a complete physical exam at the start of the race. Some teaching is done but most of these mushers have spent weeks and months training and knowing their dogs. This year there were twelve mushers who would start the 350 mile race.

Mushers leave at three-minute intervals. A fifteen minute delay means there is barking and yapping for the better part of an hour. I am often asked if it is cruel to "make the dogs run". I don't see how you could be at a start and question that. The dogs are barking, jumping in the air and totally unable to understand why their musher won't let them run. The dogs must be held back by heavy ATV's at the start.

A second race started an hour after the first race. These six entrants were 13 to 17 years old. Some would pass the "real" mushers on the trail. These mushers are very real and are the future of the sport.

Dogs and mushers travel over 350 miles and climb 6000 feet in elevations to compete in the event. This year the weather is warm. The dogs run best below 20 degrees. Unfortunately it is 35 to 45 degrees on the trail. That means the mushers cannot run during the day and they have to go slower. It also means the snow is packed and icy. Humans and animals slip and fall. The dogs that splay can pull shoulders and pull their pectoral muscles. Humans sprain backs, bruise butts and get concussions.

The mushers mostly seem to be on top of things. Some dogs come in carried in to the checkpoints in the sled bag. They are hot or sprained. Most of these dogs will be dropped to get a ride home in the truck. Some will get massaged back to racing shape. No pain killers can be used for the dogs on the trail. (Let me tell you I used plenty of Naprosyn from MY trail bag!)

Veterinarians are on hand to check dogs as they arrive. Dogs should

It's Not Just Puppies and Kittens

come in with their heads up and tails held high. In short, they should be having a good time. The mushers and the veterinarians cooperate to give the dogs the best possible care.

At the first checkpoint, the mushers all arrive within a couple of hours. Later in the race, they will be spread out. If the GPS's were all working, we would have a good idea when they would be in, but a glitch means we don't know when all will be in. So, I find myself at 2:15 am around a campfire with an experimental physicist, a boiler maker, a horse wrangler and another veterinarian who used to be a wildlife biologist.

Later all are taking a break, but a musher decides his dogs don't have it in them to continue. He turns around and heads back to the checkpoint. I am the only official around to allow him to scratch. He and his dogs will not continue on this race. Three other 350 mile mushers and one junior racer will decide the race is too much for them this time.

One musher will be in danger from dehydration because of a mistake that left behind his energy drinks. One dog will be in danger from pneumonia, but not from the cold. Another musher helps the musher in danger. Veterinarians start IV's and help the dog. Both are doing better today. Some dogs that sit on the couch will get pneumonia. People who do not push themselves will not know their limits.

And we scatter, back to our real lives until a future year, when we meet to share stories, get little sleep and work hard in bitter conditions. But we will meet again to allow the dogs to Race to the Sky, and to ensure they receive the very best of care when they do.

Seal Skin Hat

While I was at the restart of the Race to the Sky, a lady came up to me and introduced herself as an elementary school teacher. I generally appreciate the efforts of our teachers and had started to talk to her, when she started attacking my hat.

Now my hat is quite striking. It is very dark gray fur with black spots and quite unusual.

She first asked if it was seal, when I replied it was, she loudly said she had studied this with her class. The ex-wildlife biologist keyed in on what was going on way before I did.

The teacher stated my hat was a harbor seal (It is not.) and that it was awful what they do to the harbor seals. I have not been on a harbor seal hunt and I do not know what happens. I do know sometimes things are reported are not exactly reported as I see things when I am present. I do however know exactly who made my hat. But first, let me tell you how I came to have my hat. When I worked the Iditarod in 2007, it was warm when I boarded the plane in West Virginia. I arrived in Anchorage around midnight and I caught the first Piper Cub out to the trail in the morning.

That means less than 24 hours after leaving Kentucky, I was on Finger Lake in the bush of Alaska. Finger Lake is one of the coldest places around. Not only are the veterinarians sleeping on 6 feet of ice in a small tent, but there is a lodge 600 feet up on the bank. Now sleeping in a "heated tent" where ice forms inside your bivy sac between you and your sleeping pad is interesting in itself. My water bottle froze solid in the insulated bottle jacket, which was on my backpack inches from my head.)

Speaking of water, we were working so hard and it was so cold we didn't have time to thaw out the Coleman fuel. I got a dehydration headache and have a permanent inability to handle heat from my three days on Finger Lake.

Of course, psychologically knowing there was a lodge just up the bank that we were not allowed in because "we tracked," make it even colder. I got off on the last flight of the day three days later, actually just after the sun went down. Volunteer pilots for the Iditarod cannot take off from unlit "airstrips" after sundown but I certainly was not going to say anything. (In this case, the "strip" was the lake.) The fact that all of the luggage and I hit the overhead during takeoff, was not considered a big deal because I was sooooooo happy to be leaving Finger Lake.

When I arrived back in Anchorage, I begged to be allowed enough time to go buy a fur hat from the gift store at the Native Alaskan Medical Center. (Natives sell their goods to the store or on commission and any profit goes to scholarships for the Alaska natives. This is a win-win in my book.)

The only hat that fit me was a single seal skin hat with beaver trim. It was about twice what I really wanted to spend, but I quickly purchased it so I could get back and go on the trail.

It is beautiful. Mary from a village 100 miles north of Shaktulak made it for me. I provided about 3 months of subsistence living for her and her family. The seal is very light almost white when born. So my seal was an old, probably adult male. The seal meat is eaten in the village. The fact the natives eat it makes me glad I support their way of life. I have eaten seal meat and it is definitely not to my taste, but it does have this bizarre warming effect.

I do know my hat has saved my life. Not only does it protect me from painful frostbite, but it has cushioned my head when I have slipped on the ice. I take care of it and appreciate the life that gave my hat, but this hat helps me take care of the dogs that are much better suited to cold than I.

The biologist ended up giving the teacher a lecture while I watched. I wish people would educate themselves and not believe everything they are told.

Genesis 1:26 And God said, Let us make man in our image, after our likeness: and let them have dominion over the fish of the sea, and over the fowl of the air, and over the cattle, and over all the earth, and over every creeping thing that creepeth upon the earth.

My part of that job is helping care for animals, and sometimes, they get to help care for me. That seal helped me, which meant I was outside ready to help a raven with a broken wing in Unalakleet on the Iditarod trail.

It's Not Just Puppies and Kittens

Remember Y2K?

I do. Ashland Central park will. Even if they do not remember why they do. But sometimes we do things for those who have gone before, just because.

It was November of 1999 and the world wasn't too sure what was going to happen. Some said the rapture was coming or the world would end. Others said all of the computers would crash and money would become incalculable. Most thought things would go on, but nobody was quite sure.

It was November on a warm Saturday after Thanksgiving that 12,000 daffodils were planted in Central Park. Katana Bowling and I were finishing up our Master Gardener class and we had to do our projects. Most people did a church garden or taught a class at school or the prisons, but I talked Katana into doing a little more. (That was an significant understatement folks.)

When our teacher, Lori Bowling, heard what we were planning, she said it could not be done. Since I deal with the nearly impossible on a routine basis, we didn't really listen to her and soon Katana had convinced the Park Board that a field of daffodils would be a good thing and we finally had permission.

Fund raising for the Millennium Memorial Meadow was next. We sent out fliers asking for donations. I had a rather devastating pet loss that was still an open wound years later, so this was a rallying point. Some people gave money in the name of a pet or spouse or someone else important. But there wasn't enough, so I donated a $2000 to buy a lot of daffodils. (The next spring, I donated more and Kurt and Carla Jaenicke donated $1000 and then brought their staff (and families) from Ashland Women's Care to help plant 7000 more bulbs.)

Knowing we would need planters for 12,000 bulbs, Katana and I recruited help. Ernie Tucker had been vocal about needing to do some things to beautify Ashland, so we were soon pointed in his direction. Ernie rose to the occasion and helped with planning, fund raising and by giving his class extra credit, lots of planters.

Ramey-Esteep home, girl scouts and classroom children helped plant also. Some helped with fund raising. Katana and/or I taught the classes about daffodils. Daffodils are toxic so pets, squirrels and other critters won't eat them. Daffodils do well as long as they get sun, but they are up and done before the trees leaf out, so they can be planted around deciduous trees. They quickly multiply, so girl scouts have gone back out and relocated and divided daffodil clumps.

Neither Katana nor I demanded the spotlight, so we gave credit to the master gardeners, but it has rankled to see the project credited to the city of Ashland, the Park and various others in government.

This project came for a couple of reasons. The first came from a need. Steven Covey, of 7 Habits fame, says we need to have legacy (among other very important things). Regardless of other things in my life, I will have done something good. And also sometimes a memorial helps make sense of the anguish of grieving. The Millennium Memorial Meadow will live on for decades or centuries and every time I see a daffodil; I will think of Chip, the chocolate lab that died way before his time.
http://www.daffodilusa.org has a lot of good information about daffodils.

It's Not Just Puppies and Kittens

The scenes are horrifying.

An earthquake moved Japan, the axis of the world and shortened the day. Aftershocks were as powerful as major earthquakes. A tsunami erased villages. Thousands are dead. And unknown more are missing.

Specially trained dogs provide hope. This week, six canine disaster search teams arrived in Japan. These teams are trained by the National Disaster Search Dog Foundation (NDSD). They have been "deployed to disasters around the world, helping find life in the midst of devastation and death."

The NDSD Foundation uses rescued dogs and trains them. They smell and hear human life among rubble and then bark to alert their handlers. A dog's sense of smell is 1000 times greater than a human's. They can hear better because they can change the position of the outer ear or pinna to focus on a particular sound. This is like the old ear trumpets which magnified sounds. That is why dogs with triangular ears or semi-floppy ears can hear better than dogs with very long ears. Dogs also hear much higher frequencies than humans. A dog can hear 40,000 to 100,000 vibrations per second while a human can only hear about 20,000 vibrations per second.

But it is not enough to smell or hear or know there is life beneath rubble, the dogs must be trained to signal their trainers. Hours, days and weeks of training are put in. Some dogs are good, others, not so. Only the great make a team.

There are 74 SDF trained teams in the US. Six have gone to Japan this week. "All rescue personnel will be awaiting a 'Bark Alert' from the dogs, letting them know there is someone in need of rescue. Everything the teams have learned during their intensive training will be put to use in saving lives," says Janet Reineck, of the Search Dog Foundation.

Photos of the teams in action in Japan are at http://www.searchdogfoundation.org/98/html/index.html. They are true heroes and go into danger so others might live. A bark, someone is found.

And the dog gets a pat on the head, a treat and then a rest until they move on to find others. Always hoping to find others. These teams have gone into coal mine disasters, earthquake zones, mud slides and kept our hopes alive after 9/11.

Thousands are dead. And unknown more are missing. But how do they know how many are missing? If whole families are gone, who says the Lees are missing? But, the dogs don't care who is missing, they search for life. Later, other dogs will come and search for cadavers. For now Japan searches for hope. We send dogs and prayers.

The Day the World Changed

A Single solitary **moment** in time. 102 minutes overall, but focused on a single solitary moment. There are moments in time which change all of humankind. Sometimes these are for the good, sometimes not. Sometimes we know they are life changing at the time, sometimes we do not.

There is a 36 lecture course (www.thegreatcourses.com) that teaches about these moments, it is called The World Was Never the Same. The course states that to be such an event three things must happen: the event in itself fundamentally changed history; the aftermath of the event changed history; and the event and its impact still resonate with us today.

The trial of Jesus, the landing of Christopher Columbus and the falling of the world trade centers all changed history and the impacts are still resonating today.

Of silence: In the days after the attacks on the trade centers, the pentagon and flight 73, we sat in front of the TV seeing the images again and again until they were ingrained in our brains. The days at work were almost spent in a zombie state. We were doing our jobs, but not really sure what was to be next. The silence settled as no more live victims were to be found at ground zero. Tireless teams of dogs and their handlers searched, but the silence was oppressive. Of the 95 dogs that searched, 13 are still alive today. I think the dogs felt the silence, too.

For those who: There were four hijacked planes. Two headed to the world trade centers, one to the pentagon and the fourth was headed to the Capital or White House. That day, there were a total of 2,996 deaths, including the 19 hijackers and 2,977 victims. Almost everyone knew someone who died that day or at least knew someone who knew someone personally. For me, it was a young Army Captain who went on to put in 25 years and die at the pentagon that day.

Wish: In the years since we have learned to put things in perspective. We have changed, we will never be the trusting people that we once were. But I believe in the American people, I think we will overcome. Indeed, this is the reason I purchased a big building and took the financial risk. I believe the people of the United States will fix the things that need to be and rise above the current financial problems. Personally, I now take a stronger lead in volunteer activities. Where I would not have spent the time, I now will step up, because I know I can and therefore feel I should.

To pray. And the decency of the world showed in those days. People helped others get out of the trade centers. Strangers gave water to others on the street, just because there was need. Around the world, people flocked to embassies to lay wreaths, cards, flowers and other offerings. I do not believe quite the way of others and believe strongly that all should be free to believe and practice their religions as they feel they should (not hurting others of course), but on those days, it seemed everyone came together to lift up their spirits together.

Yesterday, we added a new print to the waiting room. It is a search and rescue team. The print shows the actual paw print of Aspen, one of the world's most decorated search dogs. Aspen died in 2005.

A moment
    of silence
        for those who
            wish
                to pray.

SECTION 9: HOWL-I-DAYS

The Time Changed. I Haven't Yet.

I am writing this right before we "spring forward" the clocks. By the time this is in print, I will be tired and off schedule. When I was growing up there were folks who just refused to switch their clocks from "cow time". (This was before the internet, much TV and in an area where many of these folks were still close to the farm.)

I have never stopped to think of the effect of the switch to daylight saving time (DST) on my pets. I mean, eat, sleep, repeat– what is there that an hour would affect? But if a pet is in tune with their owners' schedules, the one hour jump can cause confusion. I will admit that Half seems to panic in the fall when we are not up on time, but I thought he was just taking advantage of the opportunity to climb on my chest and be in my face while I was trying to sleep.

Animals use their internal clocks or circadian rhythm to tell them when to wake up, eat and sleep. With pets this is less about natural sunlight and more about electrical circuit completion. In other words, we set our pets' routines.

"Animals that live with humans develop routines related to human activity — for example, cows become accustomed to being milked at particular times of day, or pet dogs become accustomed to going for walks or being fed at a particular time of day," Holdhus-Small a research assistant at CSIRO Livestock Industries, an Australia-based research and development organization. "When humans apply daylight saving time to their own lives, if they carry out their routine according to the clock, the animals can become confused."

Holdhus-Small uses the milk cow as the example of why the farmers refused to use the "new" time. When the clocks fall back in the fall and the farm owner arrives an hour "later" to milk the cows, they will be at the barn, bellowing because their internal routine tells them that the farmer is late. On the other hand, in the spring, the cows will think the farmer is an hour too early and will not come to be milked until the "proper" time.

It's Not Just Puppies and Kittens

"When humans change the clocks for daylight saving, to suit our preferred working environment, from an animal's point of view, we are suddenly behaving oddly," Holdhus-Small said. "To the animals, it is inexplicable that suddenly dinner is an hour later or earlier than expected."

For the cows, it is easy to see milking an hour "late" will cause physiologic stress. But this can affect house pets, also. It is conceivable pets could be annoyed when they find an empty food bowl at "feeding time".

But unlike those farmers without corporate or public jobs, we cannot ignore daylight savings time. A good compromise therefore, might be to change a few minutes a day rather than a whole hour at once. This may alleviate some paw-holding and grumpiness, at least on the pet's part. In the meantime, be thankful you are not a school teacher trying to teach first period this week!

Background for this article was provided by Life's Little Mysteries, a sister site to LiveScience.com

Make Mine Chocolate

My best friend would love the House Rabbit Society's Easter campaign. See, she loves chocolate and, well, not so much, the care associated with pets.

The "Make Mine Chocolate" campaign was created by the Columbus, Ohio, chapter of House Rabbit Society. "Rabbits are not 'low maintenance' pets," says Margo DeMello, president of HRS. They require at least the same amount of work as a cat or dog, and often more. Chocolate rabbits are great alternatives; kids can enjoy them for 10 minutes, and they won't have to take care of them for the next 10 years."

Every year, well-meaning parents and grandparents buy cute "Easter bunnies" and other Easter critters for children. And then each year, thousands of baby rabbits, chicks, and ducks that are purchased as Easter gifts are abandoned to starve or left at shelters in the days, weeks and months that follow Easter.

It is not that rabbits don't make great pets, they do. But unless you are willing to make the commitment to care for the animal for the next ten years, they should not be purchased as pets. Also, most kids want to carry, cuddle and hold their companions, but rabbits are not meant for that. They have extra vertebrae (spines) in their lower back which allows their backs to break easily. Rabbits are usually on someone's lunch menu and therefore don't like loud noises, something kids are great at.

If you are willing to make the long term commitment, rabbits need an indoor cage that is four times their adult size. Wire bottoms can cause sores on rabbit feet, so are not recommended. The cage needs extra room for a letterbox, toys and food and water bowls. Litter should not be the clumping type or the dusty type. Wood shavings grow germs and have respiratory irritants, so are not good either.

It's Not Just Puppies and Kittens

Rabbits need lots of exercise, at least 30 hours a week in out-of-cage, but safe rabbit-proofed home area. They should never be left unattended outside. Not only do lots of things try to eat them, but they are masters of escape.

Rabbits need lots of fresh water, unlimited fresh grass hay, veggies and a small amount of pellets.

Just like dogs and cats, they should be spayed or neutered. Uterine cancer is common in unspayed females. Unneutered males spray urine all over your house. Not my idea of a great roommate!

Oh, and they shed a lot. They shed their entire coat, 3-4 times a year.

And baby rabbits, they have more accidents, take more time, do more chewing and still grow up to be rabbits. And the sweet personality changes at puberty.

Of course, dogs and cats are some work also. If you do think you might want to share your house with a rabbit (and they do make great pets just not easy ones), the shelter and rescue groups are a good place to look. Start at `www.rabbit.org` which has a lot of good information.

And if you don't want to make this commitment that is okay, just think about a chocolate rabbit for everyone on your Easter list.

It's Not Just Puppies and Kittens

Yappy Howlidays! Hold the Tinsel

Thanksgiving is safely behind us (leftovers are dangerous for pets) and at our house it is now time to decorate. I abhor the Christmas decorations in the stores in August and at our house and business, we do not start decorating until the day after turkey day.

But after the meal a few things do start coming out. Not all of our decorations leave the boxes or even the attic though. Our pets are part of our family and some holiday decorations are dangerous to pets. We have a real tree, so there will often be scents and smells that interest our four footed crew. This means we tie the tree to the top of the banister so it does not come crashing down. Pine needles can be toxic and irritating and therefore should not be eaten. Likewise Christmas tree water can have tree preservatives and irritating pine tar and should not be drank.

If your pet has any inkling toward chewing electric cords, hide the lights cords well or crate your pet when they are not attended. Flashing lights are more attractive than regular cords, so be careful.

Many pets think ornaments are toys and try to play with them. Broken glass ornaments cut paws and tongues. At our house the glass ornaments go high on the tree and there are some special pet safe ones at the bottom of the tree.

Tinsel is probably top on the danger list. Not that any of you have tried this, but think of how hard it is to get dog hair out of your mouth with fingers. Tinsel in a pet mouth is almost always swallowed. If it catches on something in the intestines, the intestines will continue to try to move it out but it just results in sawing holes in the intestines. Cats love to chew ribbon and it can do the same thing. Even with surgery this is often fatal. Angel hair can both slice intestines and cause blockages.

Poinsettias have a reputation for being toxic and they are, but not nearly as much as people think. Holly leaves, holly berries and mistletoe are also toxic. Remarkably Christmas cactuses are not.

Oh, and the presents under the tree, don't think for a second the pets don't know which ones have what type of chocolate, food or something they like to chew. The pretty paper may hide the contents from humans with their lousy senses, but dogs and cats might has well have x-ray vision when it comes to presents.

Other holidays have hazards also. In addition to Thanksgiving leftovers, Easter grass and Easter Lilies at Easter, candy at Halloween, fourth of July alcohol are all dangerous to pets.

I have to write about what I know. Our house celebrates Christmas with a tree and all the trimmings, but I am certain the holidays of other religions decorate with pet hazards also. Regardless of the holiday you celebrate, please think about all the dangers in your house for all your members. And Yappy Howlidays!

It's Not Just Puppies and Kittens

A Gift for Spot and Tabby

A poll just released by the Associated Press found over half of all Americans are going to give their pets gifts this holiday season. In case you still have shopping to do, I have a few ideas.

All indoor pets should have a stocking. Santa finds it difficult to keep the children out of the pet toys without a stocking. Remember it is difficult for pets to read, so a stocking is easier for the pet to remember after you show them.

At our house, pets get an ornament their first year. This goes on the tree that year and every year afterward. Yes, there can be tears during tree decorating time at our house. Photo frames are also used for pet pics.

There is no question dogs love to smell food under the tree. Probably best to not actually put it under the tree before present opening time. Make sure if a dog has special dietary needs that you are careful. They do make hypoallergic treats and foods.

Rawhides are a good low calorie treat, just make sure the treats are US made and salmonella or bacteria free. Rawhide can be shaped into various shapes.

Dog clothes are another popular gift. Seasonal sweaters and outfits are popular, but snow boots and jackets are useful items. Jackets are especially nice for those late night walks in the rain or snow. Seems Ranger snuggles best when he is wet. His new jacket should leave the wetness downstairs. A new collar may need to be purchased anyway and this is a good time to give it. Jewelry or personalized tags are another present option.

Most favored pets will get a toy. Squeaky toys may need to be used under supervision. There are some dog toys that are well made, but some of the cheap ones are dangerous. Well made dog toys are best, but of the cheaper toys, the best buys are in the baby section.

Any stuffed toy should be supervised and removed or repaired at the first sight of stuffing. Rope toys should always be thrown away if the

It's Not Just Puppies and Kittens

knot unties. Balls should be large enough not to be swallowed. Note a racquetball is too small for a lab. I have taken them out of throats before.

Cats love laser toys and cat fishing poles. To catnip or not to catnip is a family decision.

Older dogs have been shown to have better cognitive function later in life if they play with puzzle type toys. These puzzle toys work well for hyperactive dogs also. These toys almost always have something that has to move to get to the food. Puzzle toys can keep the pet busy for hours.

Pets that don't sleep with the humans may need a new bed. Orthopedic egg-crate foam is good for older dogs.

Pets have been shown to be good for older folks; however these folks may not always have money for pet care. Most veterinarians will work up a gift certificate for care.

The AP poll numbers are actually 56% of the dogs will get presents and 48% of the cats. I wonder which indoor cats and dogs will not get gifts? My husband says I missed getting him something one year (believe me, he remembers), but I have never missed the pets. Indeed, I have yet to get all of my shopping done, but I do have gifts for all the pets already.

What about you? Will there be something under the tree for your dogs, cats and other pets?

A Cat's Night Before Christmas

(apologies to Clement Clarke Moore)

"Twas the night before Christmas, when all through the house
Not a creature was stirring, wait did I hear a mouse?
Among the stockings by the chimney did he dare,
I mean, really? St Nicholas soon should be there!

The children were nestled all snug in their beds,
While on the mantle two mice poked out their heads.
I suspect they thought they would duck out for a quick nightcap,
Did they really think I was in for a long winter's nap?

When I moved for them, they knocked over stuff with a clatter,
I sprang to the chair to get above the splatter.
Down from upstairs my dad flew like a flash,
He looked like a shopper on a last minute dash.

It's Not Just Puppies and Kittens

Looking around the fallen objects, his anger did grow
I saw in my future a night out at eight below.
I know and I saw how things might appear,
But it wasn't my fault the mice were as clumsy as reindeer.

But now with fair warning, the mice were so quick,
I knew in a moment I would be outside to see St Nick.
More rapid than eagles my master did curse my name,
And he hollered, and shouted, and put me out in shame!

"Now Cat! now, Demon! now, Spawn of Vixen!
I feed you good food, let you sleep in my house and you go on this Blitzen!
To the back porch! Stay off the top of the wall!
Now get away! Get away! Get away from it all!"

As the husband went back in, the wife's words did fly,
When he met this obstacle, he knew he should not have told me goodbye.
So outside to find me in the snow, he flew,
I think he was most grateful, he quickly found me, too.

And then, in a twinkling, we were back under roof.
During the prancing and pawing, I acted aloof.
As I cleaned my paws, and was turning around,

It's Not Just Puppies and Kittens

Down the chimney a mouse came with a bound.

He was covered in black, from his head to his foot,
And his fur was all tarnished with ashes and soot.
It was like my Christmas toy was back,
I gave him just enough time to say "Ack."

The tree lights-how they twinkled! The music how merry!
My master buys roses, but she prefers chocolate with a cherry!
But the droll little mouse was drawn up like a bow,
And the belly and feet were as white as the snow.

I picked him up and held him tight in my teeth,
A grand idea encircled my head like a wreath.
Instead of putting this mouse in my round little belly,
That shook when I laughed, like a bowlful of jelly!

This mouse was chubby and plump, a right jolly old elf,
And I laughed when I thought this, in spite of myself!
A wink of my eye and a thought in my head,
Soon gave me to know I was headed straight to her bed.

It's Not Just Puppies and Kittens

I spoke not a word, but went straight to my work,
And padded past stockings, then decided to lurk.
I chose to lay it right beside of her nose,
With a shriek, straight out of bed she rose!

It might have been okay if the mouse hadn't given a whistle,
But he wasn't quite dead and was thrown like the down of a thistle.
But I heard Dad exclaim, 'ere I flew out of sight,
"I told you to leave that damn cat out tonight!"

It's Not Just Puppies and Kittens

(Our Christmas/Holiday letter to our clients.)

Yappy Howl-I-daze!

December 2011

Our second full year in the new location and already, it is another record year! We are STILL moving and unpacking, but are making progress. We truly feel we have become a member of the community. We were even chosen as The Ashland Independent's 2011 Reader's Choice Award for Best Veterinarian. While it is a great honor and I am very pleased, I will continue focusing on what is best for the patients; even when it means I don't win popularity contests. We continue to add those extra services little by little. I have contacted two board certified surgeons about visiting periodically. We will see what the New Year brings, but we will continue to make strides forward.

Christmas is a big thing here at GAMC, come see our three trees including one designed by Linda Johns for the Festival of Trees. It is great to have a place for a BIG Christmas tree or two or three! The extra room allows us to do photos for Santa & Paws. (Join us Dec 15 from 5 to 7pm).

Many changes are good, but a great thing that hasn't changed is that my core staff is still with me. Dennis, Casey and Stephanie have all been with me 4-5 years. Steph has grown into the team leader position and her leadership is invaluable to me. Dennis is a touchstone to me and others.

It's Not Just Puppies and Kittens

After the new year, Casey will be flexing his wings in a new position in Huntington.

In the sled dog world, I will not be using those new Michigan or Montana licenses this year, but am looking forward to going to Canada for the Hudson Bay Quest. And no, I don't know any French for the mushers from Quebec. Let's just hope their dogs are bilingual.

We are continuing to help adopt animals from the shelter and through our spay-neuter program. This year, we spayed/neutered and placed over 70 kittens in our spay/neuter program. Please do not leave animals on our door step. We don't like it, but euthanasia is often our only option. We are limited in what we can do with those animals. If you take them to the shelter, we can help from there. (BTW We have had two different animals break loose from home and come to GAMC on their own.) :)

We continue to take in hawks, owls and other wildlife for rehabilitation. We cannot come and pick something up. Remember we get no money from the state or feds, but do this as a community service. The costs of rehabilitation continue to increase. That is why, we are having photos with Santa as a fund raiser for our wildlife(Yes, we do have a donation box all year that helps.)

I am enjoying writing an article for the *Greenup Beacon* and the Sunday *Ironton Tribune*. People have stopped me on the street and at the checkout to tell me how much they enjoy my article. That means a lot. Thanks!

It's Not Just Puppies and Kittens

I update facebook daily. There are lots of tips and some just for fun things. The website, www.GuardianAnimal.com has general information for GAMC and a peer reviewed pet article library. (Be careful what you believe on the internet.) So, make sure we have your email address in our system for our quarterly newsletter.

On a personal note, Matt has been diagnosed for two years now with Inclusion Body Myositis. This is a progressive total muscle degenerative disease that has no treatment or cure. Matt will be moving his office to GAMC with the new year.

We appreciate your prayers, but please do not try to talk to me in the exam rooms about it. I find in order to survive, I must forget for a while. I am grateful for my work that allows that. However, for my life lesson to you, I would advise you do take time to dance while you can.

With all the negative things in life, I have worked hard to remember the good things. I sincerely appreciate all the clients who choose to drive further to continue to come to us. I appreciate your referrals!

The economy has hit us as much as all of you, (I will really be glad to put start up expenses behind me), but we continue to support the World Wildlife Fund, Bat Conservation International and the American Veterinary Medical Foundation.

Meowy Christmoose and Yappy Howlidays!

MJ Wixsom, DVM MS

M'Kinzy and Matt

Dennis, Casey, Stephanie, Becky Jo, Brian, Cally, Caleb, Julie, Jared and Jenny

Sid, Bunnicula, Nugget and SamRanger, Half-n-Half, Chacotay, Tequila, 'keets, turtle and fish

Roles and Goals

With the coming New Year our family sits down and does what we call roles and goals. These stem from Steven Covey's <u>Seven Habits of Highly Effective People</u>. They are not resolutions. Those get broken within the day, week or month. We work toward goals and adjust efforts as needed. Every member of our family does role and goals, even the dog.

The first habit is to be proactive. It means each individual is responsible for their own self and actions. In Ranger's case, it means he knows if he sneaks down in the middle of the night and stands on the child's step stool for cooking, he can reach and then eat anything that is left down. In other words, he is completely in charge of his extra curricular snacking.

Habit two is to begin with the end in mind. Ranger is very good at this also. Remember the time I was looking for the milk replacer and had to call my husband who was out of town to find out where it was. While I was on the phone, I repeated the location, but did not get it. That night, while visualizing his goal, he jumped over the baby gate, snuck downstairs, carefully lifted the milk off the stand and proceeded to rip the bag, eat all the contents and lick the insides clean. I am certain he had one or two obstacles in his way, but since he knew exactly what his goal was, he was able to adjust to still get the reward.

The third habit is to put first things first. I think dogs in general are pretty good at this. When you come home from a long, extended 15 minute trip, they greet you like you have been gone for weeks. You are the most important thing in their world and they let you know it. If it is doing their job or cleaning the stainless steel off the bottom of their bowl, everything gets all of their attention.

Habit four is to think win-win. I like to think of this as "win-win or no deal." Having Ranger in the house is a good deal for him and us. When he turned the stove on which started melting the plastic that had been set on a pan, he made sure to alert us before the house burned down. Okay, so he alerted when the husband did the same thing with pans out of the oven. Ranger, also, doesn't like strangers. At all!

The fifth habit is to seek first to understand, then to be understood. Dogs are extremely good at picking up on body language and pheromones. They are much, much better at picking up these nonverbal clues than spouses. Once they understand just how bad a day at work we had, they are much better at figuring out just how much to push the "I wanna go out and play."

Habit six is to synergize. Synergy is a wonderful cooperation where two or more beings come together and make something that is greater than the sum of the parts. One plus one equals more than two. Think about home defense: Ranger's hearing is much better than mine, so he alerts when there is danger (real or perceived). I have higher cognitive skill and opposable thumbs so I make a reality determination and can get my finger in the trigger guard. Therefore both of us are much safer than either would have been by themselves.

 Guardian Animal

Sharpen the saw. This means if you do not stop and take time for yourself, you will dull. Ranger could do a little better in this area because he tends to eat everything in sight and doesn't like to exercise for the sake of exercise. However, he is great about insisting I get up and do some exercise and play with him. And pet him. And be with him.

As our family is working through these habits, we know we have roles. Ranger's include being a family member, a good canine citizen and kitchen cleaner. Each of these roles have goals associated with them. A family member goal might be to get along better with his sister. A kitchen cleaner goal might be to actually wait until the items are headed toward the floor and not intended to remain on the counter or stove.

You know, I said, every member of our family does Roles and Goals, but that is not quite true. The cat does not participate.

It's Not Just Puppies and Kittens
MJ WIXSOM, DVM MS MBA

MJ Wixsom, DVM MS MBA

Dr Wixsom is a 1989 graduate of the University of Missouri at Columbia. She worked concurrently to get a Master of Science in Veterinary Parasitology. After graduation, she went back to school nights to get her MBA. She has been a practice owner since 1991 when she opened Guardian Animal Emergency Clinic. At the time she was under a covenant not to compete, so the office was open from 6 pm to 10 pm and weekends. During the days, she did relief work at two other hospitals. After two years, Guardian Animal Hospital opened full time. In May of 2009, Guardian Animal Medical Center was opened in the current location. Guardian Animal has been a AAHA accredited member hospital since the early days.

Dr Wixsom believes in state of the art progressive medicine and surgery and typically goes to over 40 hours of continuing education a year. In the area, she is seen as a veterinarian who cares and where you take your pets when they are really sick.

Before she was a veterinarian, she was LTJG MJ Wixsom, US Coast Guard. She was in the first class of women to graduate from the US Coast Guard Academy. She then served on board cutters as a deck watch officer and finally Commanding Officer of USCGC Cape Strait and then USCGC Cape Horn. She did extensive law enforcement and narcotics interdiction and search and rescue. But on the Cape Horn a 200 pound hatch broke loose and tore up her knee. Because of this injury a career at sea was not likely and she decided to go back to her childhood dream to be a veterinarian. Leadership is important to her and in the past two years she has mentored an intern and a preceptor.

The academy and the military experience left Dr Wixsom with a strong attention to duty and a duty to serve. She writes a weekly pet education column in the local Green Beacon and the neighboring Sunday Ironton Tribune. This book is from these articles. She is the standing president of the North East Kentucky Association for Gifted Education. Not only has she been a Girl Scout leader for ten years, but she was the co-Service Unit Manager and trains leaders for troop camp training.

Dr Wixsom has done wildlife rehabilitation since 1989 and has had her falconry permit although she no longer finds time to have a hawk. She now spends her field time helping survey bats in abandoned mines and caves with the National Forest Service (NFS). Late summer nights can sometimes find her wading in a pond mist netting bats with the NFS.

It's Not Just Puppies and Kittens

GAMC takes in puppies and kittens from pets that the owners have spayed. They are tested, vaccinated, spayed or neutered and adopted out. GAMC has adopted as many as 70 kittens in a season. GAMC also has worked with rescue organizations.

Dr Wixsom is responsible for year 2000 Millennium Meadow where 12,000 daffodils were planed in Ashland's Central Park for her Master Garden's project.

Dr Wixsom is a retired sled dog vet. She served as the head vet for the Race to the Sky Sled Dog Race in Montana as her 14th year of volunteering as a sled dog vet. She has been on the Iditarod trail three times and has worked at multiple races in the US and Canada. Indeed this is the main reason that she has nine state licenses and a Certificate of Qualification for Canada.

In her spare time, she homeschooled her teenage year old daughter M'Kinzy (now 15 and in college) and works on her 35 year marriage to Matthew Wixsom, attorney (also a former Coast Guard officer). She is writing a book on her time in the first class of women at CGA.

Dr. Mahesh Ambawattha

Although I have digitized photos for some chapter headings and included some from my coloring book <u>Pawsitivity</u>, all of the custom work is by the main illustrator, Dr.B.M.Ambawattha MBBS. Dr. Mahesh Ambawattha is a MBBS after finishing Medicine at Rajarata University of Sri Lanka. He is a qualified doctor from Sri Lanka working at Medical ICU - District General Hospital Matale in Sri Lanka. Not only that but also an experienced medical illustrator! He can be reached on fiverr.com as artsmate.

IF YOU WANT TO HELP

If You Want to Help

Proceeds from book sales go toward our adoptions, wildlife rehabilitation and charity work. This is expensive and Guardian Animal Medical Center cannot afford to do it all without help. Veterinary Care Foundation handles all the paperwork for our 501(c) tax deductible donations.

They can be reached at http://www.vetcarefoundation.org
Then go to donate
To a veterinary practice
Select Kentucky
Select Guardian Animal Medical Center (Flatwoods)
Select the amount you wish to donate.

Small amounts feed wildlife for a day. Large amounts provide care for an injured pet. Very large amounts allow us to do more adoptions or provide new adoption areas. You can specify what you want your donation to go to. All amounts are welcome. Just as keeping a hawk for a few weeks adds up, so do three dollar donations.

Although we would really appreciate your donation, most vets do a fair amount of charity work. Your veterinarian may also have an Guardian Angel fund.

ASK YOUR VETERINARIAN

Your veterinarian is your partner in your pet's care.

If something has made you think of a question to ask, jot it down here.

The internet is a good reference,

but Dr. Google does not know YOUR pet.

_____

_____

_____

_____

_____

_____

It's Not Just Puppies and Kittens

It's Not Just Puppies and Kittens

It's Not Just Puppies and Kittens

It's Not Just Puppies and Kittens

It's Not Just Puppies and Kittens

Dear Reader,

Thank you for reading my first book. I hope you enjoyed it as much as I enjoy teaching. <u>If you liked It's Not Just Puppies and Kittens</u>, I would appreciate it if you would help others know about it also. Recommending it to your family, friends, book clubs and children is great, but so is writing a positive review.

If you would like to email me about what you would like to see in future books, or let me know your favorite parts, please email me at sNotPup@gmail.com or on my Facebook page.

The main illustrator is Dr.B.M.Ambawattha MBBS. Mahesh Ambawattha is currently at the District General Hospital-Matale in Sri Lanka after finishing Medicine at Rajarata University of Sri Lanka. He can be reached on fiverr.com as artsmate.

There are photos of some of the patients and stories on the website www.GuardianAnimal.com

Look for sNot Pup 2 on April 28, 2016!

Hang tough,
MJ Wixsom, DVM MS MBA

www.ingramcontent.com/pod-product-compliance
Lightning Source LLC
Chambersburg PA
CBHW071315060426
42444CB00036B/2761